QUICK-AND-EASY "LITTLE FOLK" CHARTED DESIGNS

by

Georgia Lea Gorham

DOVER PUBLICATIONS, INC.
New York

Copyright © 1987 by Georgia Lea Gorham.
All rights reserved under Pan American and International
Copyright Conventions.

Published in Canada by General Publishing Company, Ltd., 30
Lesmill Road, Don Mills, Toronto, Ontario.
Published in the United Kingdom by Constable and Company,
Ltd., 10 Orange Street, London WC2H 7EG.

Quick-and-Easy "Little Folk" Charted Designs is a new work, first
published by Dover Publications, Inc., in 1987.

Manufactured in the United States of America
Dover Publications, Inc., 31 East 2nd Street, Mineola, N.Y. 11501

Library of Congress Cataloging-in-Publication Data

Gorham, Georgia Lea
    Quick-and-easy "Little folk" charted designs.

    (Dover needlework series)
    1. Cross-stitch—Patterns.   2. Canvas embroidery—Patterns.
3. Needlework—Patterns.   I. Title.   II. Series.
TT778.C76G674   1987   746.44′041   86-24358
ISBN 0-486-25342-2

INTRODUCTION

This collection of whimsical characters can be used to create an almost infinite variety of small gifts and decorations. Use a single motif to make a cheery Christmas tree ornament, package tie-on, picture, plaque, key ring, napkin ring or magnet. Repeat the same design or use several different ones together to make a pillow, a wall hanging or a rug for a child's room. On page 6 are instructions for making small stuffed dolls that can be used as ornaments, sachets or toys, and flat dolls that can be used as toys, ornaments or package tie-ons or can be glued to plaques, key rings and other items. The possibilities are limited only by your imagination.

Although these designs were originally designed for cross-stitch embroidery and needlepoint, they are easily translated into other needlework techniques. Keep in mind that the finished piece will not be the same size as the charted design unless you happen to be working on fabric or canvas that has the same number of threads per inch as the chart has squares per inch. All of the designs in this book are about the same size, averaging 22 stitches wide by 41 stitches high. The following chart lists the approximate size of the finished motif when worked on various fabrics and canvases.

Fabric or canvas	Finished size
22-count hardanger	1″ by 2″
18-count aida	1¼″ by 2¼″
14-count aida	1½″ by 3″
12-count mono canvas	1⅞″ by 3½″
11-count aida	2″ by 3¾″
10-count mono canvas	2¼″ by 4″
7-count plastic canvas	3″ by 5⅞″
5-count quick-point canvas	4½″ by 8¼″
3.5-count rug canvas	6¼″ by 11¾″

With knitting or crocheting, the size will vary according to the number of stitches per inch.

NOTES ON THE CHARTS

Each design has its own color key coded to DMC Embroidery Floss. A conversion chart for Royal Mouliné Six-Strand Embroidery Floss from Coats & Clark, and Anchor Embroidery Floss from Susan Bates appears on page 32. The colors that we list, however, are merely suggestions; you should feel free to substitute your own colors to create a design that is uniquely yours. Try stitching the basketball, baseball or football player using the colors of your favorite team, or personalize a gift for a child by matching that child's hair and eye color.

If you decide to create a new color scheme, work it out in detail before beginning the project. To get a good idea of how the finished project will look, place tracing paper over the design in the book and experiment with colored pencils on the tracing paper.

The eyes of each character are indicated by a solid black square. Select the eye color of your choice or the color of the hair or clothing of the character, avoiding light colors. For *cross-stitch*, use at least two strands of floss to make the X, then, using two strands of black floss, outline the top and the left or right side of each eye in straight stitch. For *needlepoint*, use one strand of yarn and work as for cross-stitch. Please note that on some charts a solid black square is also used to indicate a color. Do not be confused by this.

Work the nose in straight stitch and the mouth in backstitch with any dark pink or light red color, using a single strand of yarn or a double strand of floss. The colors for the eyes, mouth and nose are not given in the color key.

All outlining, indicated by solid lines on charts, is worked in backstitch, using a single strand of yarn or a double strand of floss unless otherwise indicated on the chart. Backstitch (*Diagram 1*) is worked from hole to hole and may be stitched as a vertical, horizontal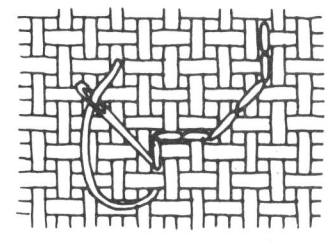

DIAGRAM 1

or diagonal line. Outlining is not always necessary on needlepoint figures except where two areas of the same color need to be defined or where the backstitching is used as trim. Where white or off-white is indicated, exterior outlining of needlepoint will be necessary only if worked on a very light background.

In *cross-stitch*, certain areas of the design are left unstitched so that the background fabric shows through. Such areas are indicated by blank boxes on the charts. The motifs were originally designed to be worked on white fabric, so blank areas are generally listed as white in the color key.

In *needlepoint*, the canvas is completely covered and blank areas on the chart should be stitched with the color indicated in the color key.

Straight stitch, lazy daisy stitch, French knots and double cross-stitch (*Diagram 2*) are used in the designs to achieve special effects. They are worked in the same manner as in regular embroidery. Unless otherwise indicated, use a single strand of yarn or a double strand of floss when working French knots.

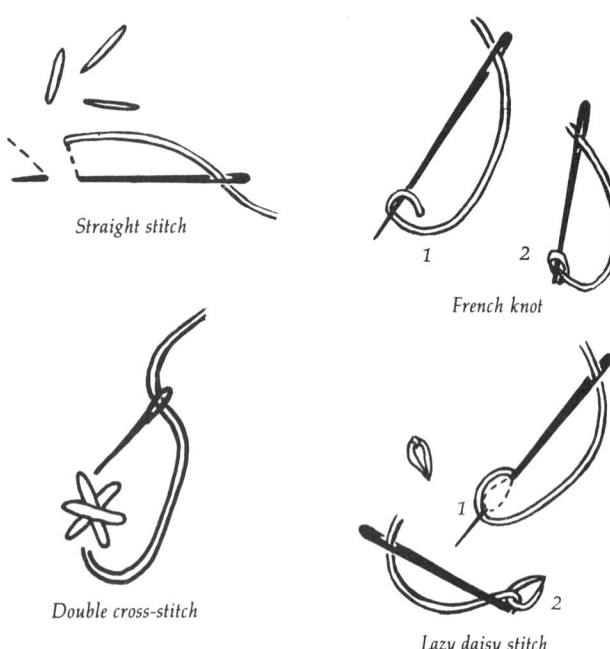

Straight stitch

French knot

Double cross-stitch

Lazy daisy stitch

DIAGRAM 2

COUNTED CROSS-STITCH

MATERIALS

1. **Needles.** A small blunt tapestry needle, No. 24 or No. 26.

2. **Fabric.** Evenweave linen, cotton, wool or synthetic fabrics all work well. The most popular fabrics are aida cloth, linen and hardanger cloth. Cotton aida is most commonly available in 18 threads-per-inch, 14 threads-per-inch and 11 threads-per-inch (14-count is the most popular size). Evenweave linen comes in a variety of threads-per-inch. To work cross-stitch on linen involves a slightly different technique (see page 5). Thirty thread-per-inch linen will result in a stitch about the same size as 14-count aida. Hardanger cloth has 22 threads to the inch and is available in cotton or linen.

3. **Threads and Yarns.** Six-strand embroidery floss, crewel wool, Danish Flower Thread, pearl cotton or metallic threads all work well for cross-stitch. Crewel wool works well on evenweave wool fabric. Danish Flower Thread is a thicker thread with a matte finish, one strand equaling two of embroidery floss.

4. **Embroidery Hoop.** A wooden or plastic 4", 5" or 6" round or oval hoop with a screw-type tension adjuster works best for cross-stitch.

5. **Scissors.** A pair of sharp embroidery scissors is essential to all embroidery.

PREPARING TO WORK

To prevent raveling, either whip stitch or machine-stitch the outer edges of the fabric.

Locate the exact center of the chart. Establish the center of the fabric by folding it in half first vertically, then horizontally. The center stitch of the chart falls where the creases of the fabric meet. Mark the fabric center with a basting thread.

It is best to begin cross-stitch at the top of the design. To establish the top, count the squares up from the center of the chart, and the corresponding number of holes up from the center of the fabric.

Place the fabric tautly in the embroidery hoop, for tension makes it easier to push the needle through the holes without piercing the fibers. While working continue to retighten the fabric as necessary.

When working with multiple strands (such as embroidery floss) always separate (strand) the thread before beginning to stitch. This one small step allows for better coverage of the fabric. When you need more than one thread in the needle, use separate strands and do not double the thread. (For example: If you need four strands, use four separated strands.) Thread has a nap (just as fabrics do) and can be felt to be smoother in one direction than the other. Always work with the nap (the smooth side) pointing down.

For 14-count aida and 30-count linen, work with two strands of six-strand floss. For more texture, use more thread; for a flatter look, use less thread.

EMBROIDERY

To begin, fasten the thread with a waste knot and hold a short length of thread on the underside of the work, anchoring it with the first few stitches. When the thread end is securely in place, clip the knot.

To stitch, push the needle up through a hole in the fabric, cross the thread intersection (or square) on a left-to-right diagonal (*Diagram 3*). Half the stitch is now completed.

DIAGRAM 3

Next, cross back, right to left, forming an X (*Diagram 4*).

DIAGRAM 4

DIAGRAM 5

Work all the same color stitches on one row, then cross back, completing the X's (*Diagram 5*).

Some needleworkers prefer to cross each stitch as they come to it. This method also works, but be sure all of the top stitches are slanted in the same direction. Isolated stitches must be crossed as they are worked. Vertical stitches are crossed as shown in *Diagram 6*.

DIAGRAM 6

At the top, work horizontal rows of a single color, left to right. This method allows you to go from an unoccupied space to an occupied space (working from an empty hole to a filled one), making ruffling of the floss less likely. Holes are used more than once, and all stitches "hold hands" unless a space is indicated on the chart. Hold the work upright throughout (do not turn as with many needlepoint stitches).

When carrying the thread from one area to another, run the needle under a few stitches on the wrong side. Do not carry thread across an open expanse of fabric as it will be visible from the front when the project is completed.

To end a color, weave in and out of the underside of the stitches, making a scallop stitch or two for extra security (*Diagram 7*). When possible, end in the same direction in which you were working, jumping up a row if necessary. This prevents

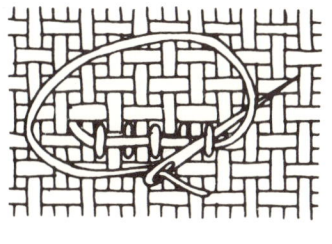

DIAGRAM 7

holes caused by stitches being pulled in two directions. Trim the thread ends closely and do not leave any tails or knots as they will show through the fabric when the work is completed.

Embroidery on Linen. Working on linen requires a slightly different technique. While evenweave linen is remarkably regular, there are always a few thick or thin threads. To keep the stitches even, cross-stitch is worked over two threads in each direction (*Diagram 8*).

DIAGRAM 8

Embroidery on Gingham. Gingham and other checked fabrics can be used for cross-stitch. Using the fabric as a guide, work the stitches from corner to corner of each check.

Embroidery on Uneven-Weave Fabrics. If you wish to work cross-stitch on an uneven-weave fabric, baste a lightweight Penelope needlepoint canvas to the material. The design can then be stitched by working the cross-stitch over the double mesh of the canvas. When working in this manner, take care not to catch the threads of the canvas in the embroidery. After the cross-stitch is completed, remove the basting threads. With tweezers remove first the vertical threads, one strand at a time, of the needlepoint canvas, then the horizontal threads.

NEEDLEPOINT

One of the most common methods for working needlepoint is from a charted design. By simply viewing each square of a chart as a stitch on the canvas, the patterns quickly and easily translate from one technique to another.

MATERIALS

1. **Needles.** A blunt tapestry needle with a rounded tip and an elongated eye. The needle must clear the hole of the canvas without spreading the threads. For No. 10 canvas, a No. 18 needle works best.

2. **Canvas.** There are two distinct types of needlepoint canvas: single-mesh (mono canvas) and double-mesh (Penelope canvas). Single-mesh canvas, the more common of the two, is easier on the eyes as the spaces are slightly larger. Double-mesh canvas has two horizontal and two vertical threads forming each mesh. The latter is a very stable canvas on which the threads stay securely in place as the work progresses. Canvas is available in many sizes, from 5 mesh-per-inch to 18 mesh-per-inch, and even smaller. The most common canvas size is 10 to the inch.

3. **Yarns.** Persian, crewel and tapestry yarns all work well on needlepoint canvas.

PREPARING TO WORK

Allow ¾" to 1" blank canvas all around. Bind the raw edges of the canvas with masking tape or machine-stitched double-fold bias tape.

For any guidelines you wish to draw on the canvas, take care that your marking medium is waterproof. Nonsoluble inks, acrylic paints thinned with water so as not to clog the mesh, and waterproof felt-tip pens all work well. If unsure, experiment on a scrap of canvas.

When working with multiple strands (such as Persian yarn) always separate (strand) the yarn before beginning to stitch. This one small step allows for better coverage of the canvas. When you need more than one piece of yarn in the needle, use separate strands and do not double the yarn. For example: If you need two strands of 3-ply Persian yarn, use two separated strands. Yarn has a nap (just as fabrics do) and can be felt to be smoother in one direction than the other. Always work with the nap (the smooth side) pointing down.

For 5 mesh-to-the-inch canvas, use six strands of 3-ply yarn; for 10 mesh-to-the-inch canvas, use three strands of 3-ply yarn.

STITCHING

Cut yarn lengths 18" long. Begin needlepoint by holding about 1" of loose yarn on the wrong side of the work and working the first several stitches over the loose end to secure it. To end a piece of yarn, run it under several completed stitches on the wrong side of the work.

There are hundreds of needlepoint stitch variations, but tent stitch is universally considered to be *the* needlepoint stitch. The most familiar versions of tent stitch are half-cross stitch, continental stitch and basket-weave stitch.

Half-cross stitch (*Diagram 9*) is worked from left to right. The canvas is then turned around and the return row is again stitched from left to right. Holding the needle vertically, bring

DIAGRAM 9

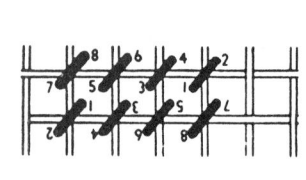

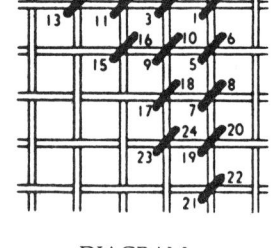

DIAGRAM 10   DIAGRAM 11

it to the front of the canvas through the hole that will be the bottom of the first stitch. Keep the stitches loose for minimum distortion and good coverage. Half-cross stitch is best worked on a double-mesh canvas.

Continental stitch (*Diagram 10*) begins in the upper right-hand corner and is worked from right to left. The needle is slanted and always brought out a mesh ahead. The resulting stitch appears as a half-cross stitch on the front and as a slanting stitch on the back. When the row is complete, turn the canvas around to work the return row, continuing to stitch from right to left.

Basket-weave stitch (*Diagram 11*) begins in the upper right-hand corner with four continental stitches (two stitches worked horizontally across the top and two placed directly below the first stitch). Work diagonal rows, the first

slanting up and across the canvas from right to left, and the next down and across from left to right. Moving down the canvas from left to right, the needle is in a vertical position; working in the opposite direction, the needle is horizontal. The rows interlock, creating a basket-weave pattern on the wrong side. If the stitch is not done properly, a faint ridge will show where the pattern was interrupted. On basket-weave stitch, always stop working in the middle of a row, rather than at the end, so that you will know in which direction you were working.

FINISHING TECHNIQUES

STUFFED CROSS-STITCH DOLL

This method cannot be used for needlepoint because canvas is too stiff to turn smoothly when working with pieces this small.

To begin, cut a rectangle of fabric at least ¾" larger all around than the size of the finished doll; overcast or zigzag stitch the raw edges of the fabric to prevent raveling. Embroider the doll following the chart. Press the stitched piece from the wrong side.

To make a hanging ornament, cut a short length of narrow ribbon or decorative cord, fold to make a loop and, with the ends of the loop up, pin it to the center top of the figure.

For the backing, cut a piece of muslin or broadcloth the same size as the evenweave fabric. Place the pieces right sides together with the cord loop inside. Using a pale-colored thread and allowing about ⅛" of fabric (2 to 4 threads depending on the thread-count of the fabric) outside the stitched outline of the doll, baste as follows: Start about ½" (6 to 11 threads) below the motif, baste up one side, around the top and down the other side to ½" below the doll. Using a stitch length of 12 stitches to the inch, carefully machine-stitch along the basted line. Remove the basting thread and trim the excess fabric 2 to 4 threads outside the stitching line. Carefully clip all corners and clip the seam allowance around the curves every ¼". Turn the doll right side out and "press" by smoothing the fabric with your fingers. Stuff lightly with polyester fiberfill. Turn in the bottom edge, leaving 2 to 4 threads of fabric showing below the feet; slip-stitch closed.

To make a stand for the doll, use a small pin-on drapery hook. Bend the pointed end of the hook so that it is perpendicular to the curved section and insert it into the seam between the feet of the doll. Adjust the curved section as needed to balance the doll.

FLAT DOLL

Cut canvas or fabric at least ¾" larger all around than size of stitched doll. Bind edges of canvas with masking tape; zigzag stitch or overcast edges of fabric. Stitch doll following chart. For needlepoint, fill in small areas such as between legs of doll with white stitching.

When stitching is complete, turn piece wrong side up and, with thumbtacks, tack canvas or fabric border to a small piece of wood, spacing tacks no more than 1" apart and gently pulling piece into correct shape.

Cut a piece of felt the same size as the canvas or fabric. With a small brush, spread white glue smoothly over the back of the needlepoint or embroidery, being careful not to get glue on the blank canvas or fabric outside the motif. Press the felt down onto the glue and allow the glue to dry for several hours. Remove the tacks. Cut away the excess canvas or fabric, being very careful not to cut away the excess felt. Glue gold or silver cord slowly and neatly around the edge of the figure onto felt, making a small loop at the center top if the doll is to be used as an ornament. Overlap the ends of the cord neatly at one side. When the glue is dry, cut away the excess felt.

Make a stand as for the stuffed doll, inserting the point of the hook between the canvas or fabric and the felt.

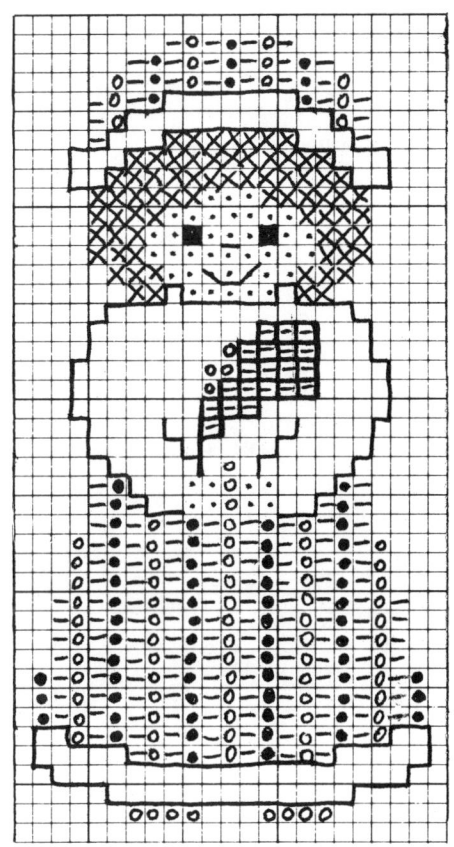

◀ BETSY ROSS

DMC #

☒	318	Light Steel Gray
◉	321	Christmas Red
⦁	754	Light Peach
◎	824	Very Dark Blue
⊟		White
☐		White

Outline large areas of White with 824 Very Dark Blue; outline flag with 321 Christmas Red.

UNCLE SAM ▶

DMC #

☒	318	Light Steel Gray
■	310	Black
◉	321	Christmas Red
⦁	754	Light Peach
◎	824	Very Dark Blue
⊟		White

Outline lower edge of hat brim with 321 Christmas Red.

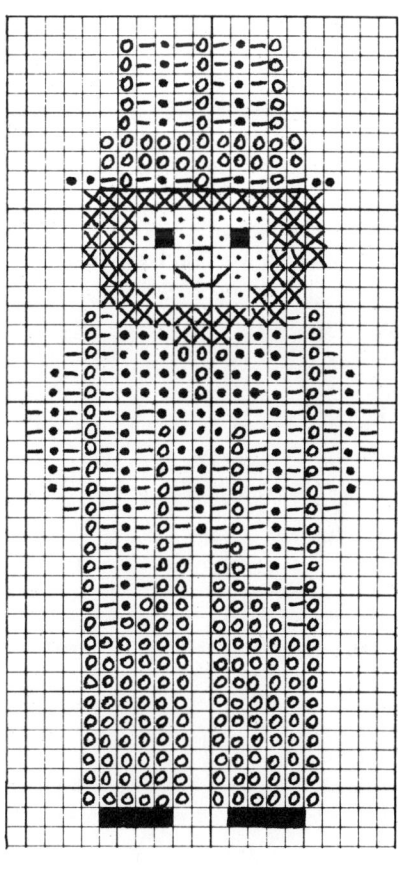

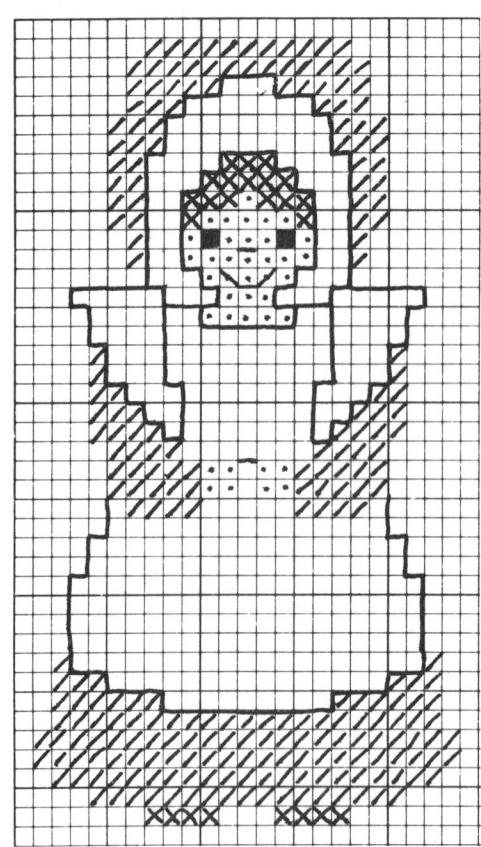

◀ PRAIRIE GIRL

DMC #

☒	434	Light Brown
—	740	Tangerine backstitch
◪	742	Light Tangerine
⊡	754	Light Peach
☐		White

Work all outlining with 740 Tangerine.

INDIAN MAID ▶

DMC #

☑	434	Light Brown
☒	838	Very Dark Beige Brown
⊡	437	Light Tan
◉	666	Bright Christmas Red
●	666	Bright Christmas Red French knots
⊟ {	666	Bright Christmas Red
	743	Dark Yellow

*see note

*For cross-stitch and needlepoint, work cross-stitches, working one half of each stitch with 666 Bright Christmas Red, other half with 743 Dark Yellow.

Outline sleeves with 666 Bright Christmas Red, spine of feather with 743 Dark Yellow.

COWBOY ▶

DMC #

◙	321	Christmas Red
◉	420	Dark Hazelnut Brown
⊞	433	Medium Brown
☒	801	Dark Coffee Brown
⊡	754	Light Peach
☑	782	Medium Topaz

Outline hat and sleeve detail with 321 Christmas Red. To make lasso, thread needle with 801 Dark Coffee Brown. Bring needle up through fabric at mark on left hand. Loop thread twice, then reinsert needle at same mark. Anchor lasso by taking a small stitch over outer loop at mark on right hand.

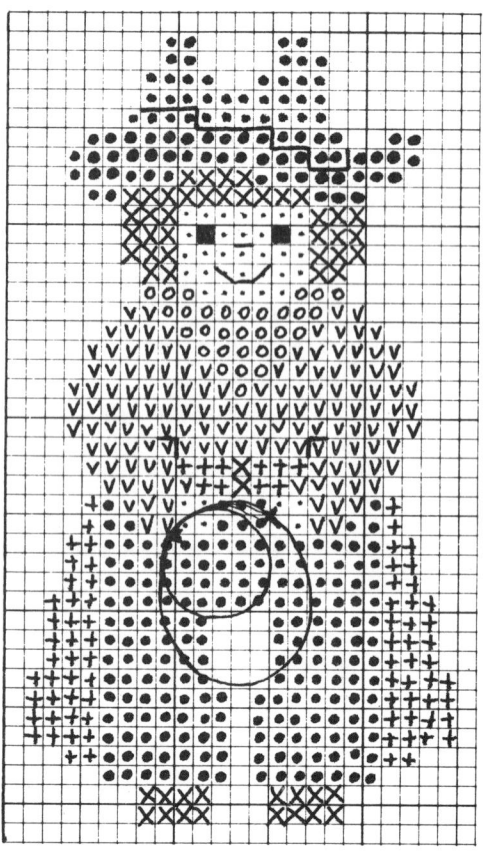

PIRATE ▶

DMC #

◉	310	Black
⌒	310	Black backstitch
☒	435	Very Light Brown
◎	666	Bright Christmas Red
⊡	754	Light Peach
—		Metallic Gold backstitch
☐		White

Outline bandanna with 666 Bright Christmas Red, shirt and eyepatch with 310 Black and treasure box with Metallic Gold.

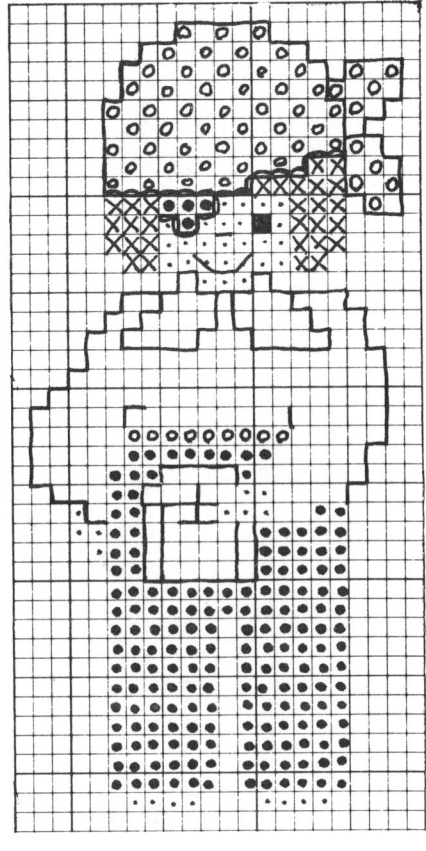

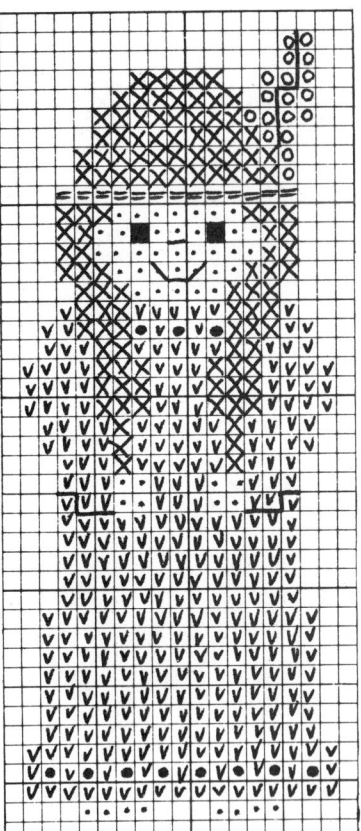

FARMER ▶

DMC #

—	310	Black backstitch
◎	317	Pewter Gray
◉	666	Bright Christmas Red
⊟	729	Medium Old Gold
⌒	741	Medium Tangerine backstitch
⊡	754	Light Peach
☒	801	Dark Coffee Brown
☐		White

Outline center of hat brim with 666 Bright Christmas Red, lower edge with 801 Dark Coffee Brown and bucket with 310 Black. Outline shirt and work solid lines in shirt in backstitch with 666 Bright Christmas Red; work remaining lines in shirt in backstitch with 741 Medium Tangerine.

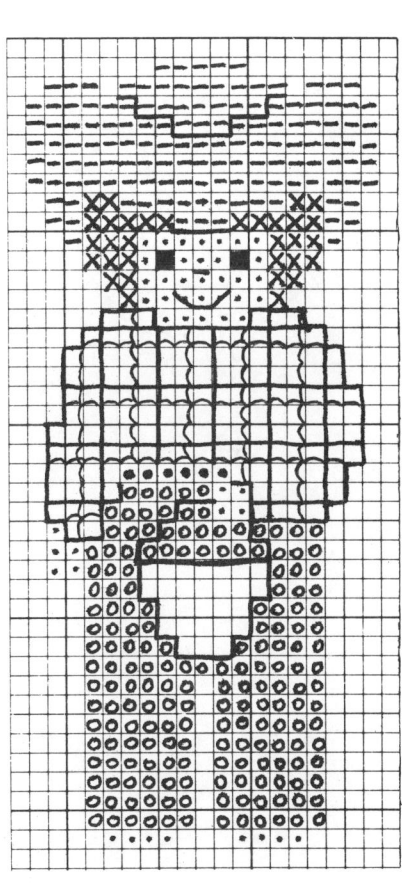

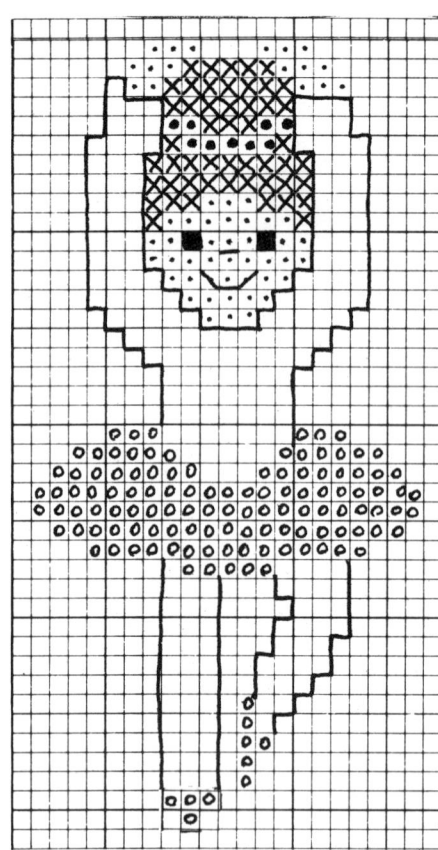

◄ BALLERINA

DMC #

- ☒ 434   Light Brown
- ⊡ 754   Light Peach
- ⊙ 962   Medium Dusty Rose
- ◉   Metallic Silver
- ☐   White

Outline leotard with 962 Medium Dusty Rose.

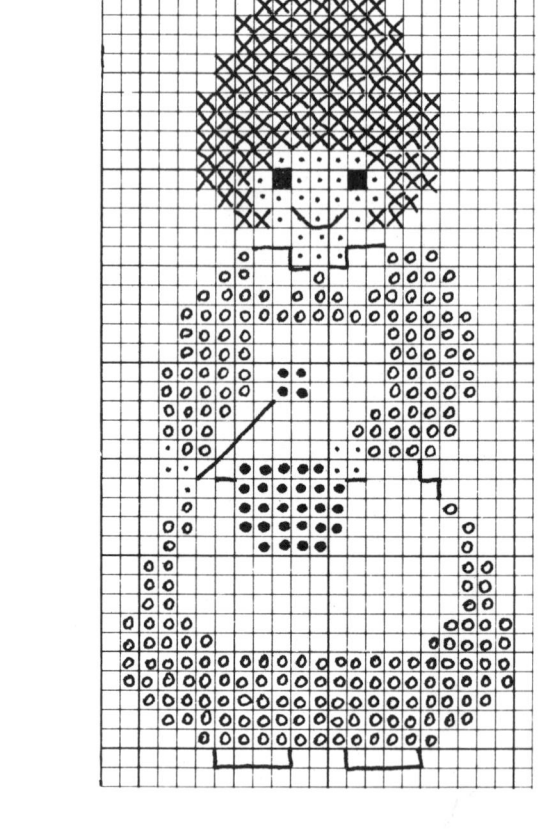

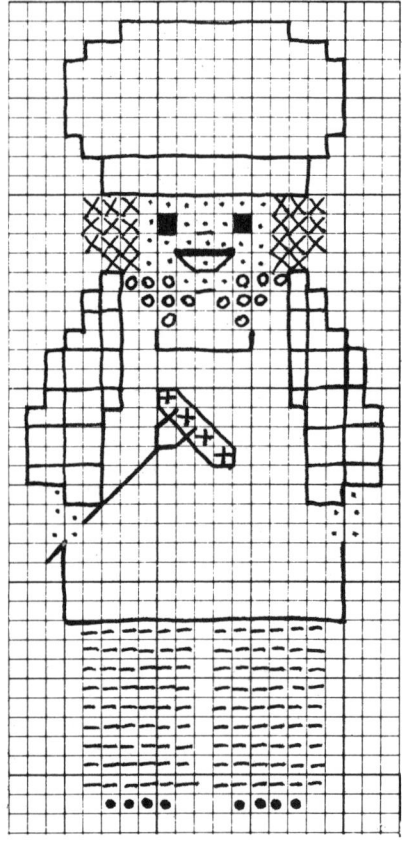

◄ CHEF

DMC #

- ◉ 310   Black
- ⊞ 351   Coral
- ⊙ 666   Bright Christmas Red
- ⊟ 452   Medium Shell Gray
- ☒ 611   Dark Drab Brown
- ⊡ 754   Light Peach

Outline hat, apron and shirt and work lines in shirt in backstitch with 666 Bright Christmas Red. Outline hot dog with 351 Coral and fork with 310 Black. Work mustache in straight stitch with 611 Dark Drab Brown.

NURSE ▶

DMC #

- ◉ 666   Bright Christmas Red
- ⊡ 754   Light Peach
- ☒ 838   Very Dark Beige Brown
- ☐   White

Work all outlining with 666 Bright Christmas Red.

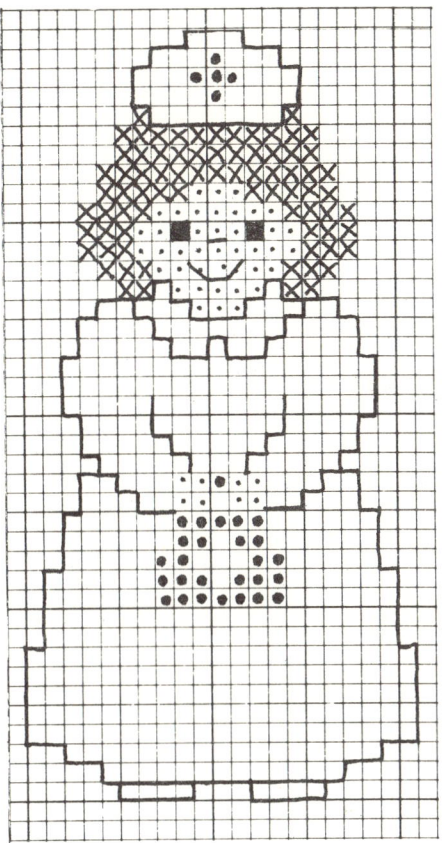

◀ COOK

DMC #

- ☒ 434   Light Brown
- ◉ 518   Light Wedgwood Blue
- ⊡ 754   Light Peach
- ◎ 891   Dark Carnation Pink
- ☐   White

Work handles of pot and spoon in backstitch with 518 Light Wedgwood Blue; outline collar, apron and shoes with 891 Dark Carnation Pink.

Bouquet Detail

◀ GARDENER

DMC #

- ☒ 433   Medium Brown
- ◎ 518   Light Wedgwood Blue
- ⊡ 754   Light Peach
- ◉ 844   Ultra Dark Beaver Gray
- ✳ 893   Light Carnation Pink double cross-stitch
-     907   Light Parrot Green
- ☐   White

Outline shirt and collar with 518 Light Wedgwood Blue. Work garden tiller in backstitch with 844 Ultra Dark Beaver Gray. After all other stitching has been completed, work bouquet in right hand following detail. Work stems in straight stitch and leaves in lazy daisy stitch with 907 Light Parrot Green.

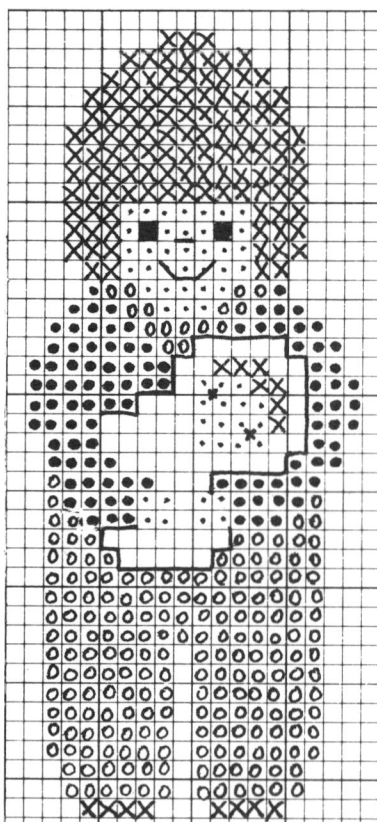

◀ FATHER

DMC #

☒	433	Medium Brown
⊡	754	Light Peach
⊙	824	Very Dark Blue
◉	827	Very Light Blue

☐ { 760 Salmon / or / White }

Use 760 Salmon or White for baby. If White is used, outline with 760 Salmon. Make French knots where indicated for eyes.

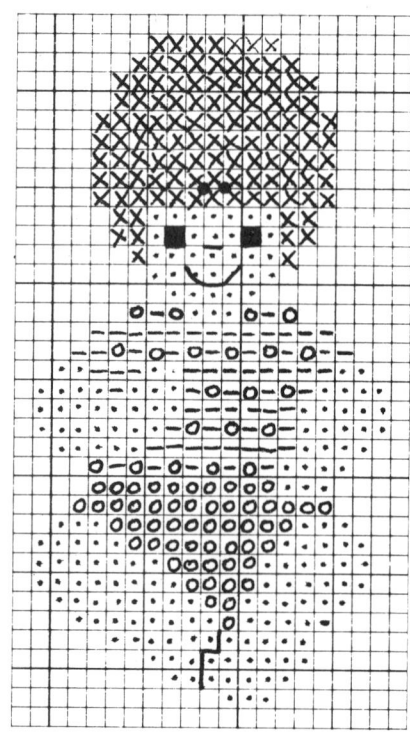

BABY GIRL ▲

DMC #

☒	839	Dark Beige Brown
⊙	893	Light Carnation Pink
⊟	894	Very Light Carnation Pink
⊡	948	Very Light Peach

Work line between feet in backstitch with 893 Light Carnation Pink. For bow, thread needle with a single strand of 893 Light Carnation Pink. Leaving long ends of thread on front of work, insert needle into fabric at one dot above forehead and back out at other dot. Tie ends of thread in a bow.

◀ MOTHER

DMC #

☒	433	Medium Brown	—— 3328	Medium Salmon
⊡	754	Light Peach		backstitch
⊘	760	Salmon	☐	White
	827	Very Light Blue		

Outline collar and sleeves with 3328 Medium Salmon. Use 827 Very Light Blue or White for baby. If White is used, outline with 827 Very Light Blue. Make French knots where indicated for eyes.

GRANDPA ▶

DMC #

☒	318	Light Steel Gray	◉	434	Light Brown
—	334	Medium Marine		725	Topaz
		Blue backstitch	⊡	754	Light Peach
⊟	336	Navy Blue	☐		White
◎	347	Dark Salmon			

Outline shirt and work French knot buttons with 334 Medium Marine Blue. With 725 Topaz, outline pocket watch in straight stitch and work French knot in center.

▼ BABY BOY

DMC #

☒	420	Dark Hazelnut	✛	893	Light Carnation
		Brown			Pink French knot
◉	825	Dark Blue	⊡	948	Very Light Peach
☑	827	Very Light Blue			

Work line between feet in backstitch with 825 Dark Blue. For "rattle," make two French knots with 893 Light Carnation Pink where indicated on left hand.

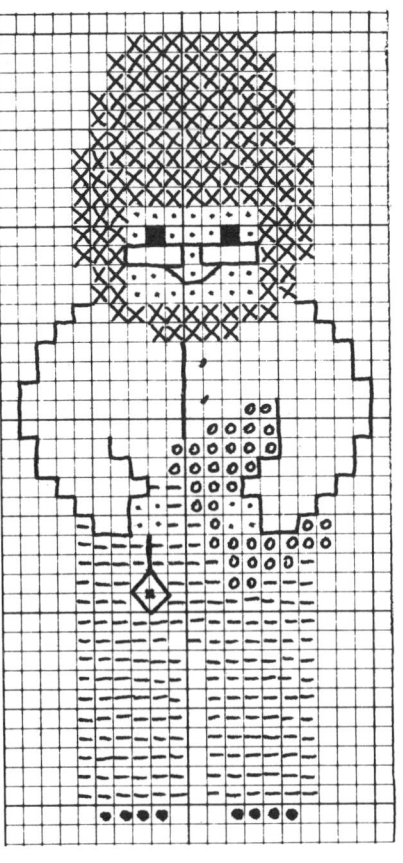

GRANDMA ▶

DMC #

⊞	311	Medium Navy Blue	—	3371	Black Brown
☒	318	Light Steel Gray			backstitch
◉	321	Christmas Red	☐		White
⊡	754	Light Peach			

Outline eyeglasses with 3371 Black Brown, dress with 311 Medium Navy Blue. Work knitting needles in straight stitch with a double strand of 318 Light Steel Gray; add a Light Steel Gray French knot at top of each needle.

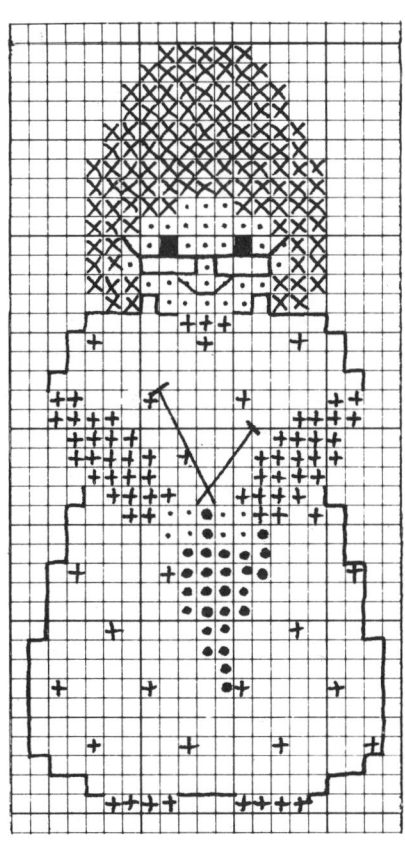

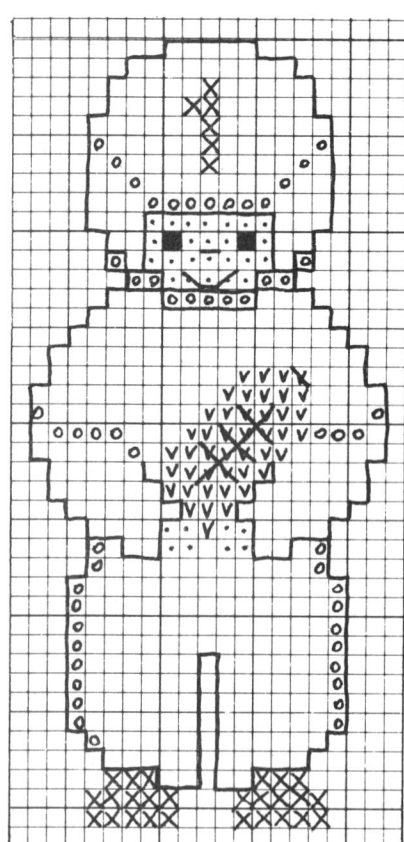

◀ FOOTBALL PLAYER

DMC #

	310	Black straight stitch
☑	434	Light Brown
⊙	725	Topaz
⊡	754	Light Peach
☒	797	Royal Blue
☐		White

Outline helmet and uniform with 797 Royal Blue. Work detail on football in straight stitch with 310 Black.

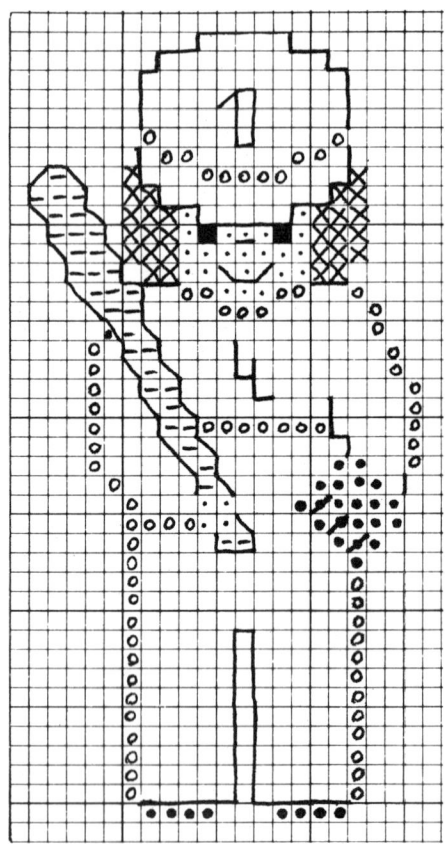

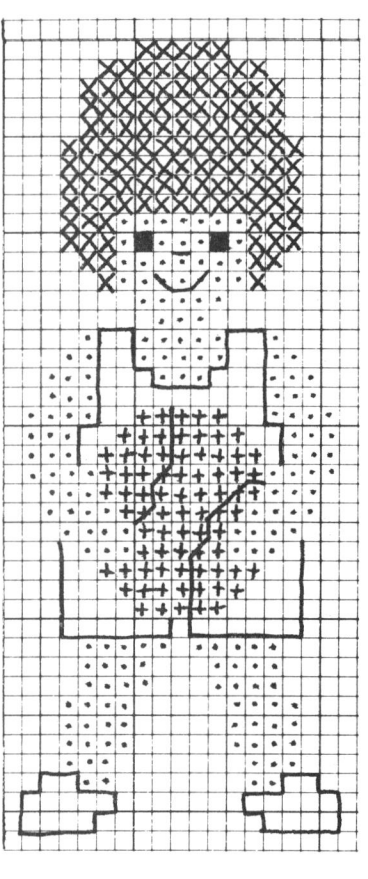

◀ BASKETBALL PLAYER

DMC #

	310	Black straight stitch
⊞	434	Light Brown
☒	729	Medium Old Gold
⊡	754	Light Peach
☐ {	824	Very Dark Blue
		or
		White

Use 824 Very Dark Blue or White for uniform and shoes. If White is used, outline with 824 Very Dark Blue. Work detail on basketball in straight stitch with 310 Black.

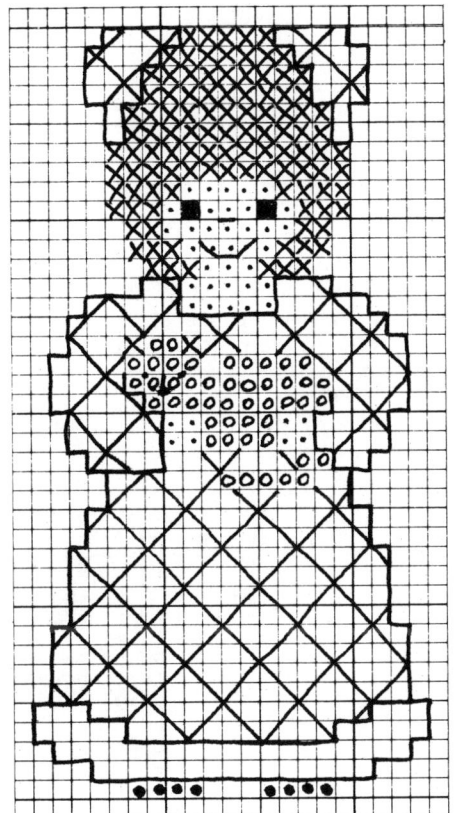

◄ GIRL WITH CAT

DMC #

	350	Medium Coral straight stitch
⊡	754	Light Peach
☒	780	Very Dark Topaz
⊙	783	Christmas Gold
⬤	912	Light Emerald Green
□		White

Outline dress, bow and checks on dress and bow with 912 Light Emerald Green. Work cat's mouth and nose in straight stitch with 350 Medium Coral; work French knots for eyes with 780 Very Dark Topaz.

◄ BASEBALL PLAYER

DMC #

⊙	310	Black
☒	420	Dark Hazelnut Brown
⬤	433	Medium Brown
⊟	437	Light Tan
⊡	754	Light Peach
□		White

Outline bat with 437 Light Tan, uniform and cap with 310 Black. Work detail on glove in straight stitch with 310 Black.

GIRL IN PINK ►

DMC #

⊟	223	Medium Shell Pink
⊙	224	Light Shell Pink
∞	224	Light Shell Pink backstitch
☒	611	Dark Drab Brown
⊡	754	Light Peach
□		White

Outline dress and sleeves with 223 Medium Shell Pink. Work stripes in backstitch with 224 Light Shell Pink.

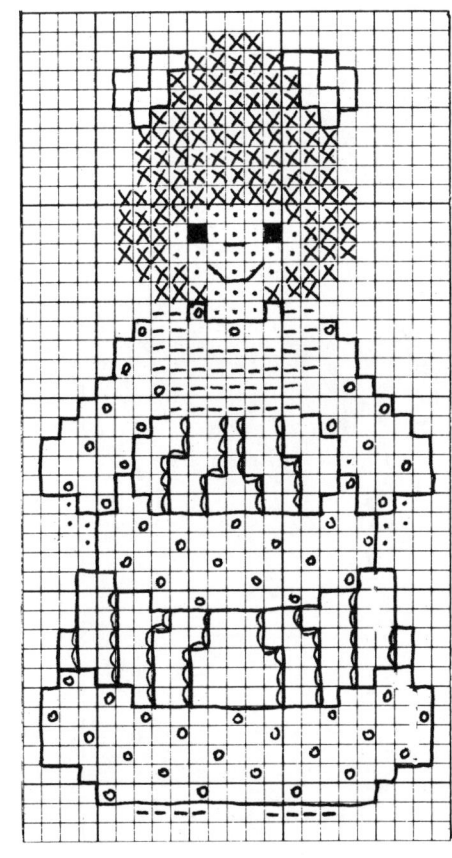

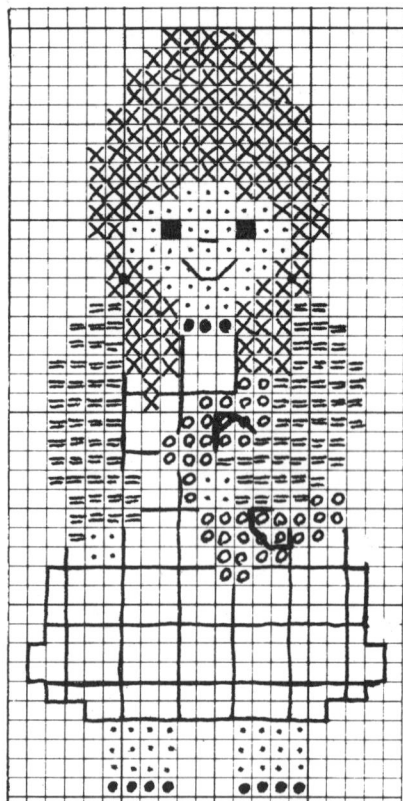

◄ SCHOOLGIRL

DMC #

⊠	783	Christmas Gold
⊙	799	Medium Delft Blue
◉	892	Medium Carnation Pink
⊟	894	Very Light Carnation Pink
⊡	948	Very Light Peach
☐		White

Using 892 Medium Carnation Pink, outline dress and checks in dress and work straight stitch lettering on book. For hair bows, thread needle with 892 Medium Carnation Pink. Leaving long ends of thread on front of work, insert needle into fabric on far side of stitch to left of dot on pigtail and back out on far side of stitch to right of dot; tie ends of thread in a bow. Repeat on other pigtail.

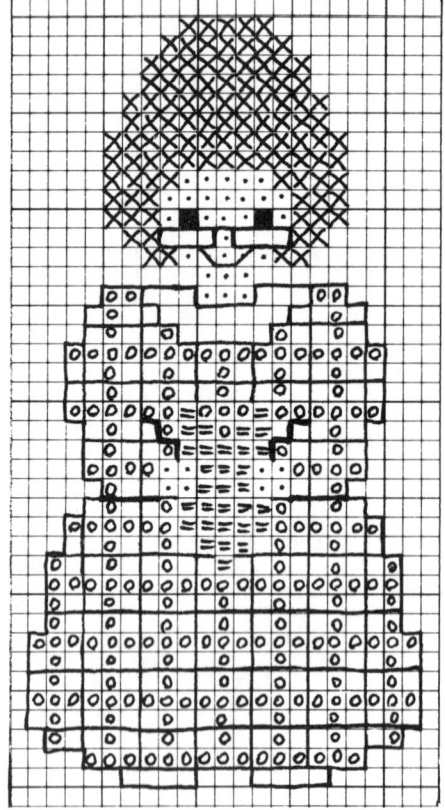

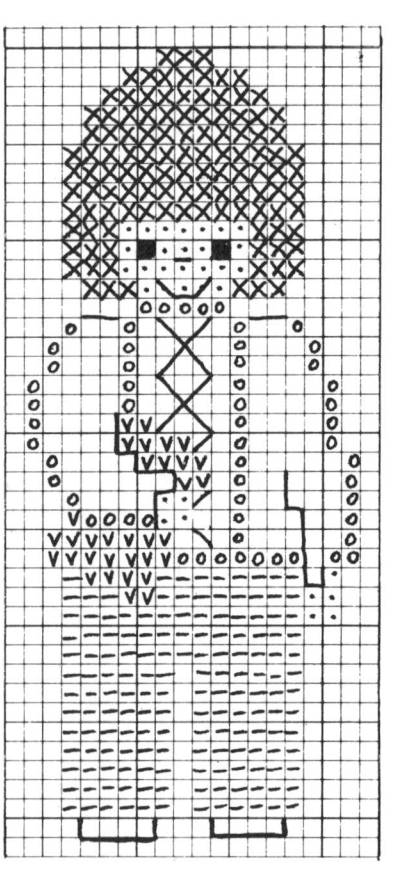

◄ SCHOOLBOY

DMC #

☑	350	Medium Coral
⊠	420	Dark Hazelnut Brown
⊟	824	Very Dark Blue
☐	825	Dark Blue / or / White
⊡	945	Light Apricot
⊙		Ecru

Outline sweater and shoes with Ecru. Work "cable" down center of sweater in straight stitch with a single strand of Ecru.

BOY WITH BOAT ▶

DMC #

☒	434	Light Brown
⊟	517	Medium Wedgwood Blue
⊚	666	Bright Christmas Red
—	742	Light Tangerine backstitch
☑	743	Dark Yellow
⊡	754	Light Peach
☐		White

Outline sail with 666 Bright Christmas Red, collar and shirt with 742 Light Tangerine.

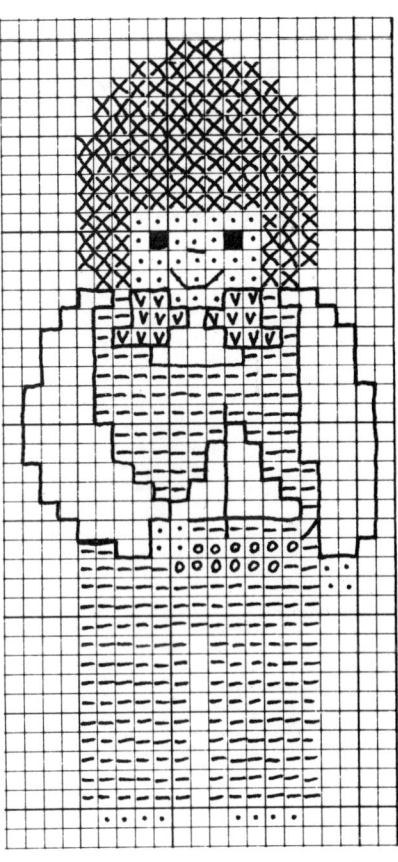

◀ TEACHER

DMC #

—	310	Black backstitch
⊟	347	Dark Salmon
⊚	351	Coral
⊡	437	Light Tan
☒	3371	Black Brown
☐		White

Outline dress, collar and shoes with 351 Coral, sleeves with 3371 Black Brown and eyeglasses with 310 Black.

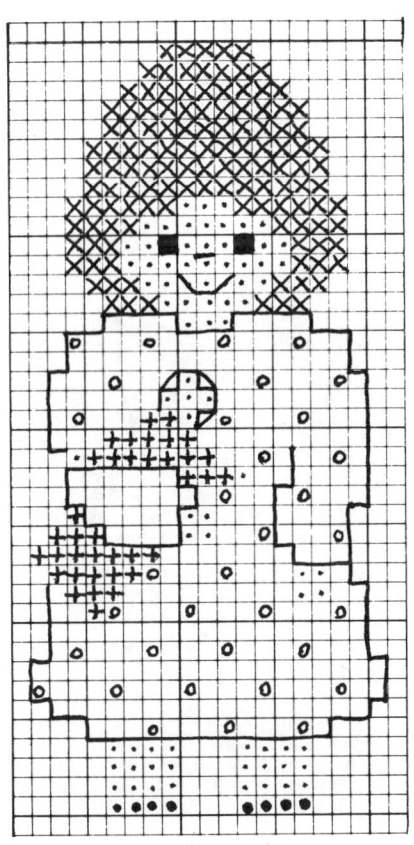

◀ GIRL WITH DOLL

DMC #

☒	434	Light Brown	
⊡	754	Light Peach	
⊚	726	Light Topaz	} *see note
	912	Light Emerald Green	
◉	912	Light Emerald Green	
⊞	962	Medium Dusty Rose	
☐		White	

*For cross-stitch and needlepoint, work cross-stitches, working one half of each stitch with 726 Light Topaz, other half with 912 Light Emerald Green.
  Outline dress with 962 Medium Dusty Rose, doll's hair with 434 Light Brown.

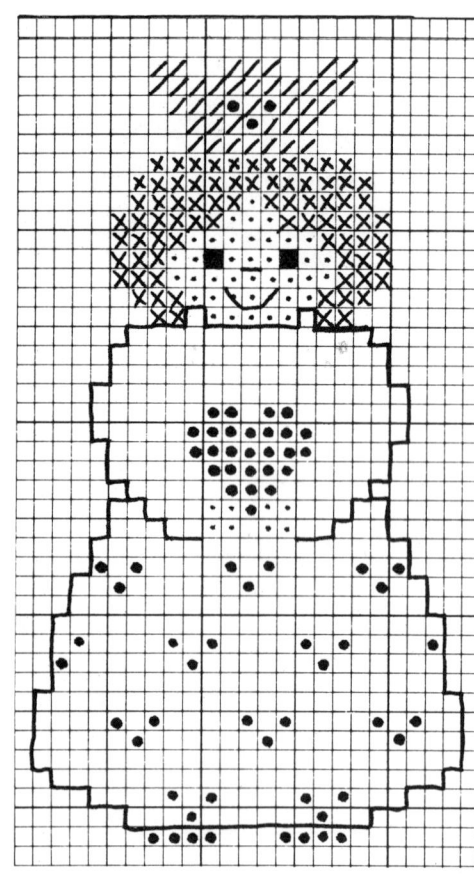

◀ **QUEEN OF HEARTS**

DMC #

⊙	321	Christmas Red
·	754	Light Peach
⧄	783	Christmas Gold
⊠	839	Dark Beige Brown
☐		White

Outline dress with 321 Christmas Red.

MISS HAWAII ▶

DMC #

⊙	347	Dark Salmon
·	754	Light Peach
⊠	801	Dark Coffee Brown
⊟	892	Medium Carnation Pink
☐		White

Outline dress and flower and work French knot in center of flower with 347 Dark Salmon.

KING OF HEARTS ▶

DMC #

⊙	321	Christmas Red
⊠	434	Light Brown
·	754	Light Peach
⧄	783	Christmas Gold
☐		White

Outline sleeves with White, border on robe with 321 Christmas Red.

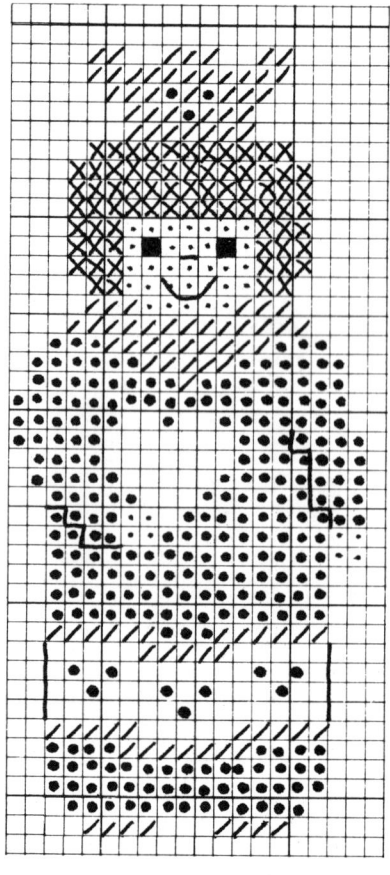

LEPRECHAUN ▶

DMC #

☑	369	Pale Pistachio Green
◉	702	Kelly Green
⊡	754	Light Peach
⊞	824	Very Dark Blue
☒	919	Red Copper
☐		White

Outline collar and sleeves with 702 Kelly Green.

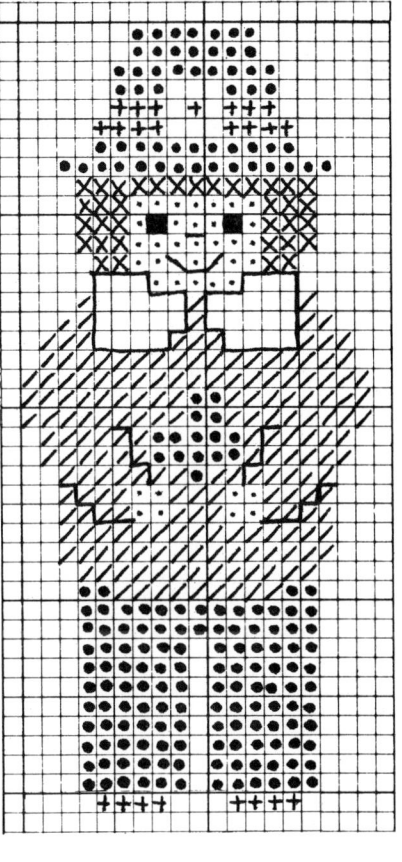

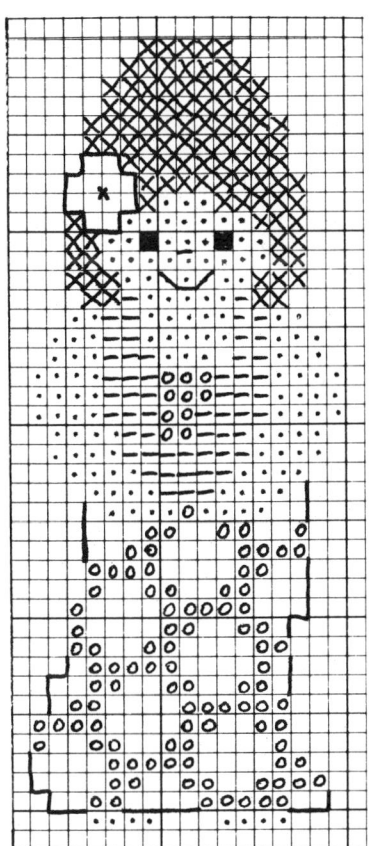

IRISH COLLEEN ▶

DMC #

☑	369	Pale Pistachio Green
◉	702	Kelly Green
⊡	754	Light Peach
☒	919	Red Copper
☐		White

Outline collar, sleeves and cap with 702 Kelly Green.

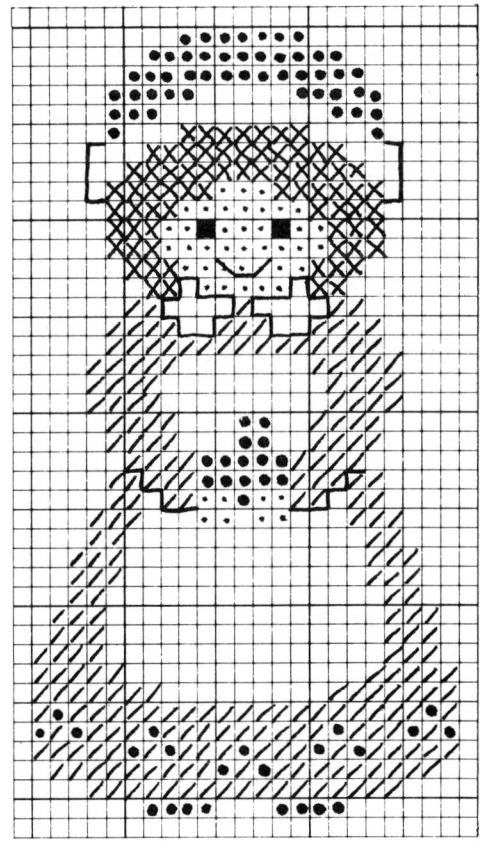

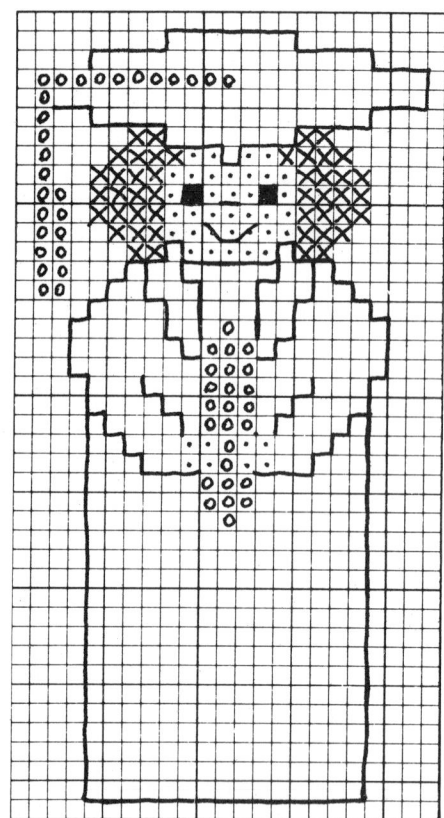

◄ GIRL GRADUATE

DMC #

☒	436	Tan
⊡	754	Light Peach
⊙	783	Christmas Gold
—	824	Very Dark Blue backstitch
☐		White

Work all outlining with 824 Very Dark Blue.

HAPPY NEW YEAR ►

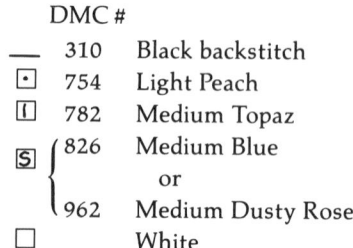

DMC #

—	310	Black backstitch
⊡	754	Light Peach
Ⓘ	782	Medium Topaz
Ⓢ	{ 826	Medium Blue
	or	
	962	Medium Dusty Rose
☐		White

Outline banner and work lettering in backstitch with a single strand of 310 Black. Outline arms and legs with 826 Medium Blue or 962 Medium Dusty Rose.

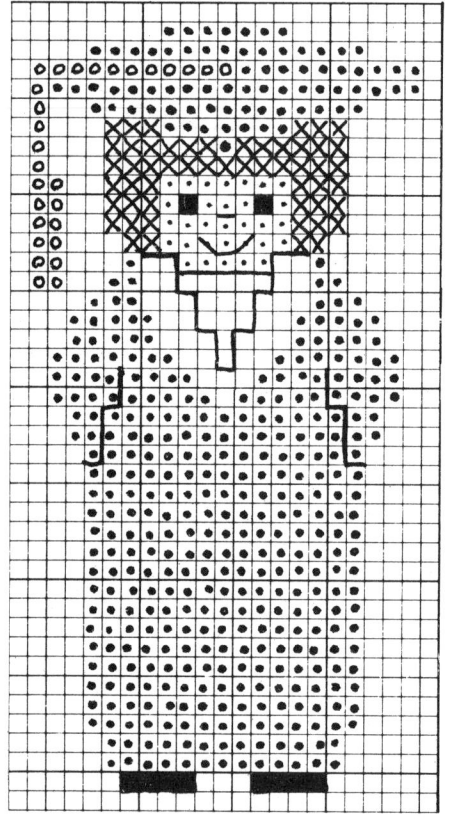

◄ BOY GRADUATE

DMC #

■	310	Black
☒	433	Medium Brown
⊡	754	Light Peach
⊙	783	Christmas Gold
⬤	824	Very Dark Blue
☐		White

Outline collar with 824 Very Dark Blue, sleeves with White.

GROOM ▶

DMC #

⊙	310	Black
	352	Light Coral French knots
⊘	414	Dark Steel Gray
☒	433	Medium Brown
⊡	754	Light Peach
	907	Light Parrot Green
☐		White

Work all outlining with 310 Black. For boutonniere, make French knots on left lapel with 352 Light Coral; work straight stitch leaves with 907 Light Parrot Green.

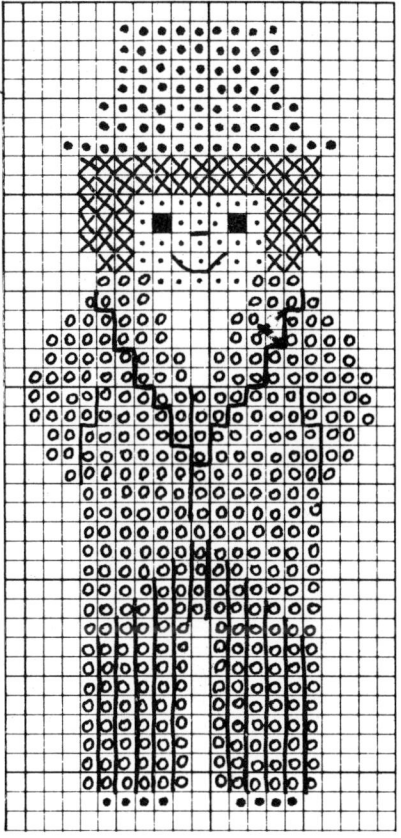

BRIDE ▶

DMC #

◥	211	Light Lavender French knots
L	352	Light Coral French knots
☒	433	Medium Brown
⊡	754	Light Peach
—	827	Very Light Blue backstitch
⊟	907	Light Parrot Green
☐		White
		Metallic Silver

Outline dress and veil with 827 Very Light Blue. For bouquet, make French knots with 211 Light Lavender and 352 Light Coral. For streamers, tie a knot in one end of each of three 3″-long lengths of Metallic Silver thread and insert free ends through piece from back at base of bouquet.

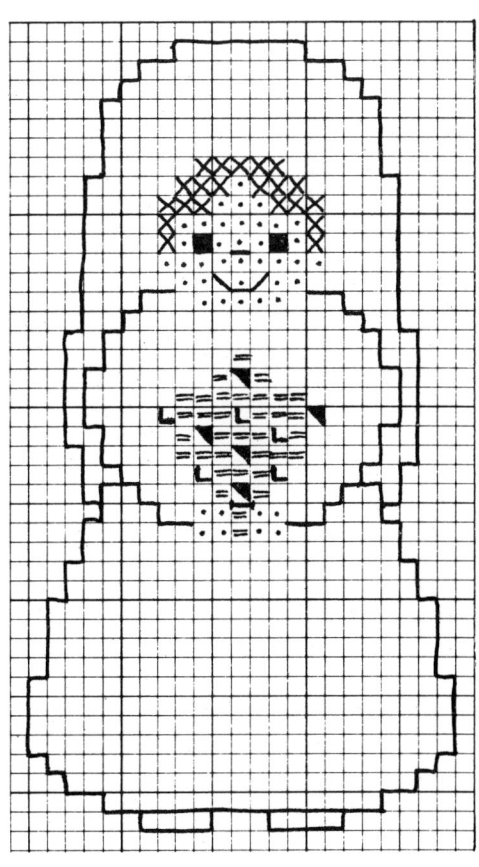

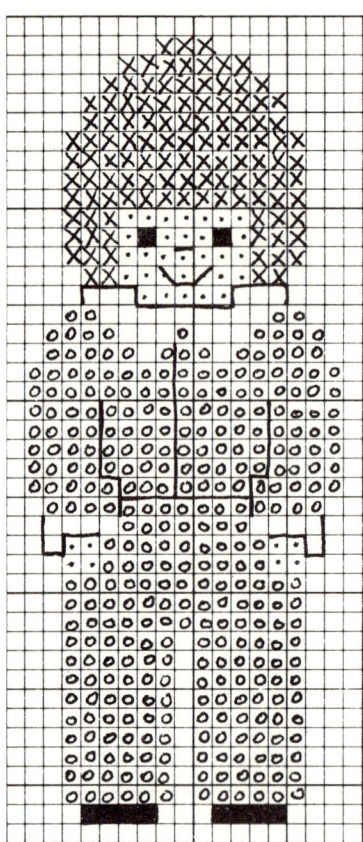

◄ LITTLE LORD FAUNTLEROY

DMC #

	310	Black
▣	517	Medium Wedgwood Blue
·	754	Light Peach
⊠	919	Red Copper
☐		White

Outline collar and cuffs with 517 Medium Wedgwood Blue, sleeves and jacket front with White.

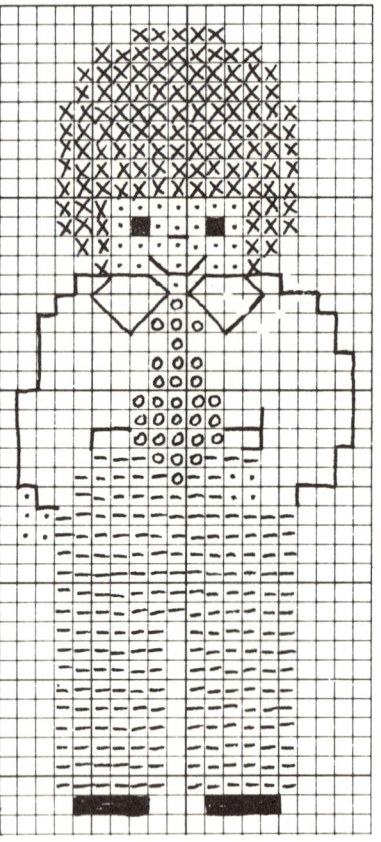

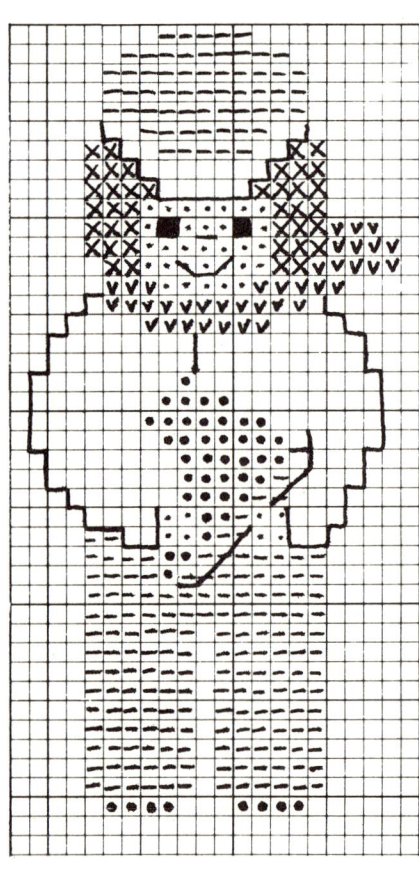

◄ ICE SKATER

DMC #

⊟	334	Medium Marine Blue
◉	336	Navy Blue
⊠	611	Dark Drab Brown
·	754	Light Peach
☑	3685	Dark Mauve
☐		White

Outline jacket and cap with 334 Medium Marine Blue, skate blade with 336 Navy Blue.

GIRL IN BLUE ▶

DMC #

☒	729	Medium Old Gold
⊡	754	Light Peach
◉	799	Medium Delft Blue
◎	800	Pale Delft Blue
☐		White

Outline sleeves and ruffles with 800 Pale Delft Blue. For hair bow, thread needle with 800 Pale Delft Blue. Leaving long ends of thread on front of work, insert needle into fabric at one dot above forehead and back out at other dot; tie ends of thread in a bow.

◀ SUNDAY BEST

DMC #

■	310	Black
⊟	611	Dark Drab Brown
☒	680	Dark Old Gold
⊡	754	Light Peach
◎	815	Medium Garnet Red
☐		White

Outline shirt, collar and belt with 611 Dark Drab Brown.

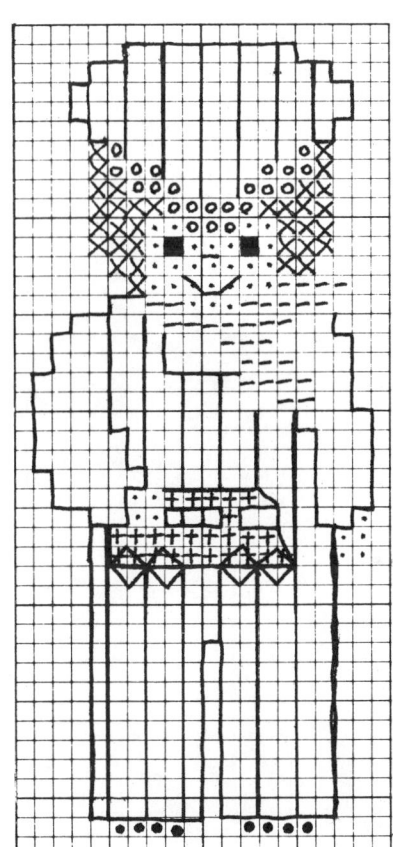

◀ ENGINEER

DMC #

◉	310	Black
☒	433	Medium Brown
⊞	666	Bright Christmas Red
⊡	754	Light Peach
⊟	815	Medium Garnet Red
◎	932	Light Antique Blue
☐		White

Outline cap, shirt and overalls and work stripes in backstitch with 932 Light Antique Blue. Outline engine and three back windows with a single strand of 666 Bright Christmas Red; outline front window with a single strand of 310 Black.

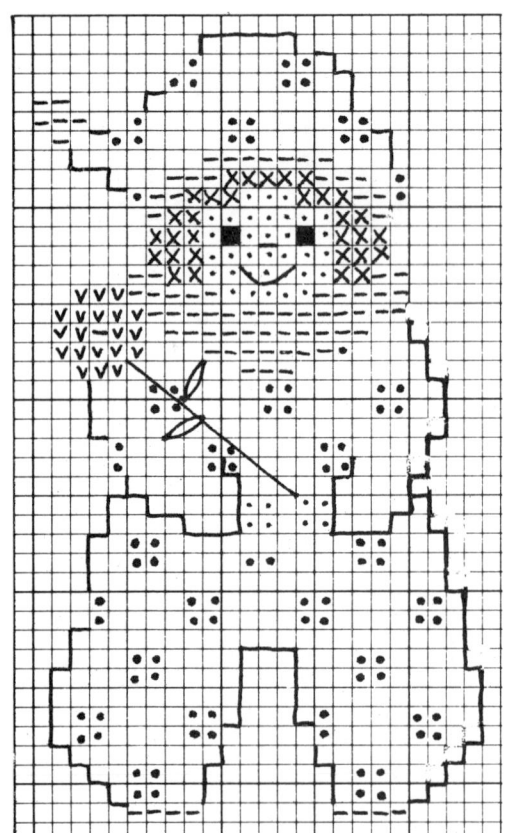

◀ GIRL CLOWN

DMC #
☒	321	Christmas Red
◉	322	Light Marine Blue
☑	725	Topaz
☐	740	Tangerine
		or
		White
⊡	754	Light Peach
⊟	907	Light Parrot Green

Work clown suit and hat in 740 Tangerine or White; outline with the other color. Work straight stitch stem and lazy daisy stitch leaves with 907 Light Parrot Green.

TENNIS PLAYER ▶

DMC #
—	310	Black backstitch
◎	312	Light Navy Blue
☒	433	Medium Brown
◉	435	Very Light Brown
⊡	754	Light Peach
☐		White
⊟		White French knot

Outline shirt and shoes with 312 Light Navy Blue, sunglasses with 310 Black and racket with 435 Very Light Brown. For racket strings, work long, horizontal straight stitches with 435 Very Light Brown, then weave vertical stitches over and under the horizontal stitches.

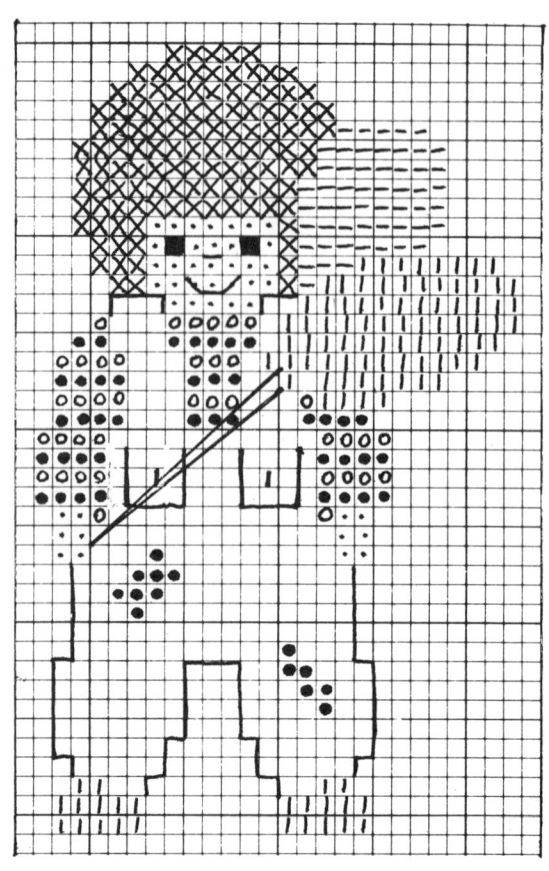

BOY CLOWN ▶

DMC #
☐	208	Very Dark Lavender
		or
		White
—	310	Black straight stitch
⊞	321	Christmas Red
◎	322	Light Marine Blue
◉	725	Topaz
☒	740	Tangerine
⊡	754	Light Peach
⊟	907	Light Parrot Green

Work clown suit in 208 Very Dark Lavender or White. If White is used, outline with 208 Very Dark Lavender. If Lavender is used, outline pockets with White. Work balloon strings in straight stitch with 310 Black.

BOY GOLFER ▶

DMC #

■	310	Black
⊠	433	Medium Brown
·	754	Light Peach
◉	825	Dark Blue
⊟	906	Medium Parrot Green
⧄		White
⊗		White French knot

Outline collar and sleeves with 825 Dark Blue. Work club handle in straight stitch with 433 Medium Brown.

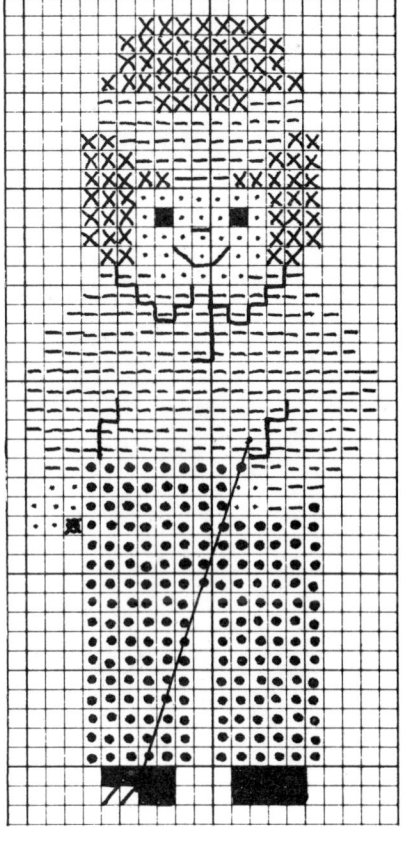

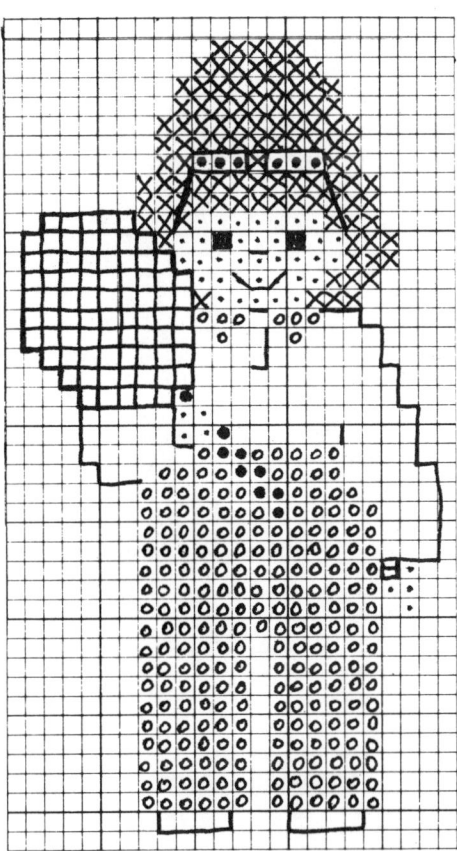

GIRL GOLFER ▶

DMC #

⊘	352	Light Coral
⩔	353	Peach
·	948	Very Light Peach
⊠	433	Medium Brown
☐		White
⧄		White
⊗		White French knot

Outline collar and sleeves with 352 Light Coral. Work club handle in straight stitch with 433 Medium Brown.

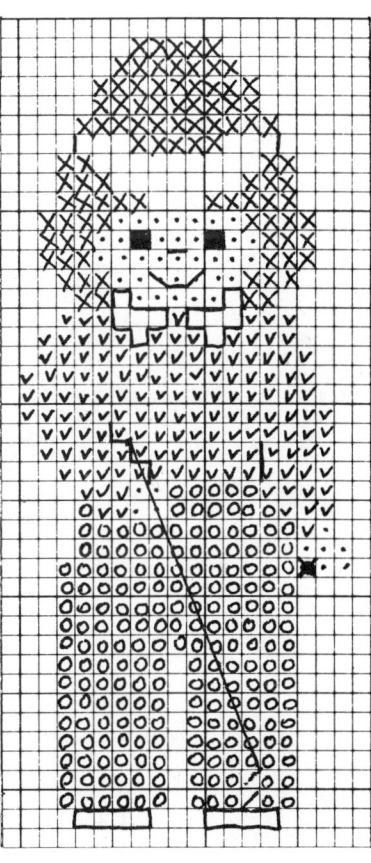

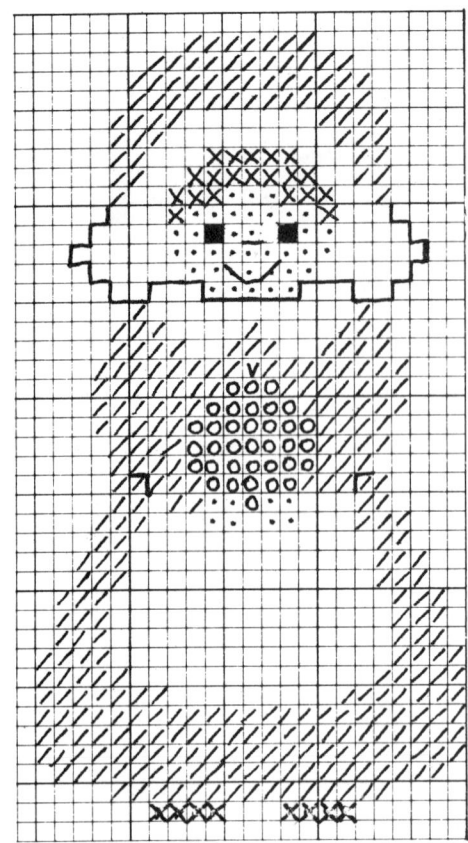

◄ PILGRIM GIRL

DMC #

☑	700	Bright Christmas Green
⊙	740	Tangerine
·	754	Light Peach
☒	975	Dark Golden Brown
⧄	3045	Dark Yellow Beige
☐		White

Outline top of collar and lower edge of hat with 3045 Dark Yellow Beige.

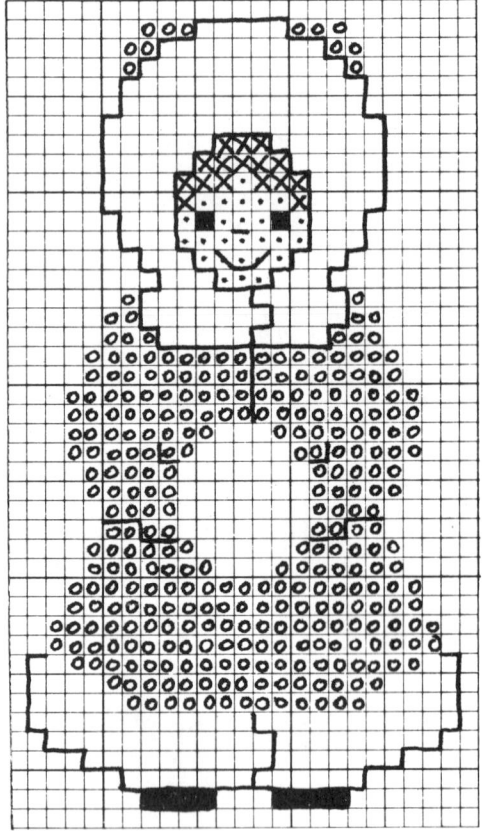

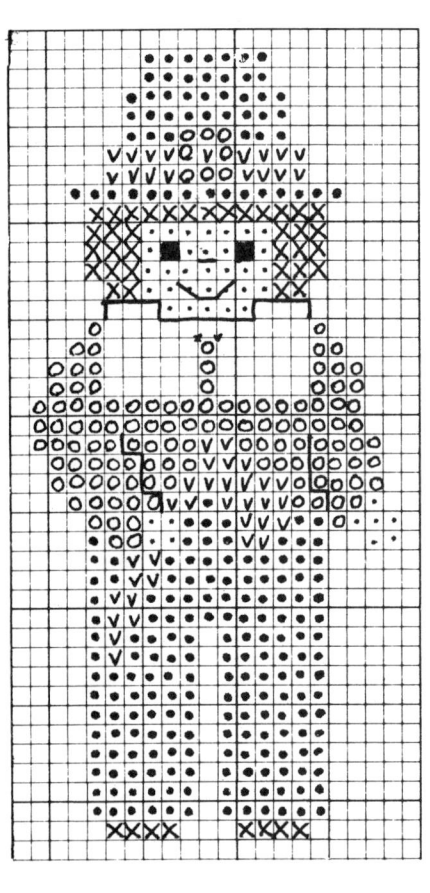

◄ PILGRIM BOY

DMC #

☑	700	Bright Christmas Green
⊙	740	Tangerine
·	754	Light Peach
●	975	Dark Golden Brown
☒	3045	Dark Yellow Beige
☐		White

Outline top of collar with 740 Tangerine. For bow, thread needle with 975 Dark Golden Brown. Leaving long ends of thread on front of work, insert needle into fabric at one dot on collar and back out at other dot; tie ends of thread in a bow.

SCARECROW ▶

DMC #
- □ 311   Medium Navy Blue
- ⊡ 369   Pale Pistachio Green
- ⊡ 677   Very Light Old Gold
- ⊟ 783   Christmas Gold
- ✱ 783   Christmas Gold French knot
- ☒ 919   Red Copper
- ⊙ 3072   Very Light Beaver Gray

Outline hatband with 311 Medium Navy Blue, overalls with 783 Christmas Gold.

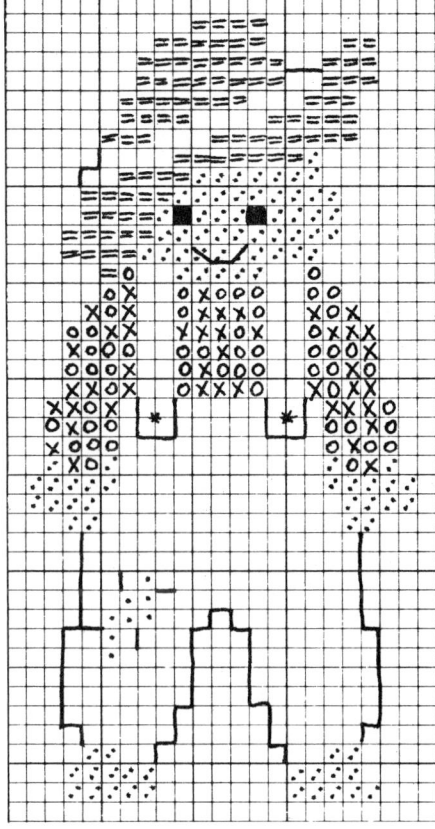

◀ WINTER WONDERLAND

DMC #
- ■ 310   Black
- ☒ 611   Dark Drab Brown
- ⊡ 754   Light Peach
- ⊙ 3687   Mauve
- □   White

Outline "fur" with 3687 Mauve, sleeves and center front of coat with White.

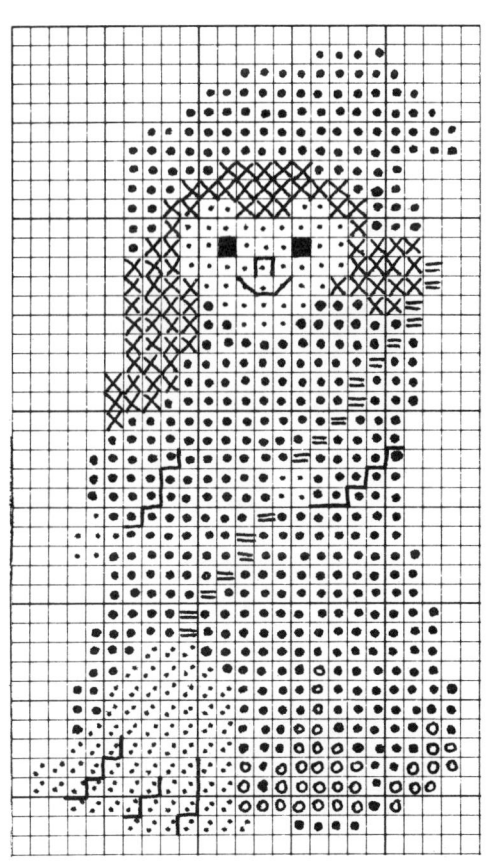

◀ WITCH

DMC #
- ◉ 310   Black
- — 311   Medium Navy Blue backstitch
- ⊡ 369   Pale Pistachio Green
- ⊡ 677   Very Light Old Gold
- ⊟ 783   Christmas Gold
- ☒ 919   Red Copper
- ⊙ 3072   Very Light Beaver Gray

Outline sleeves with 311 Medium Navy Blue, broom with 783 Christmas Gold.

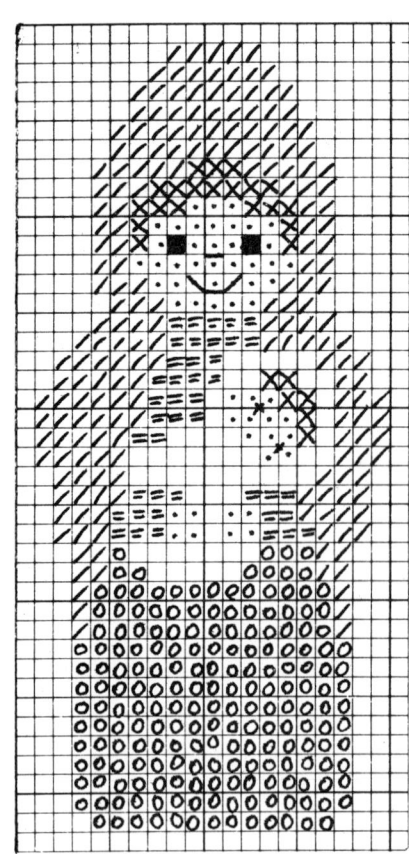

◄ MARY

DMC #

⊡	754	Light Peach
☒	801	Dark Coffee Brown
⊙	824	Very Dark Blue
⊟	826	Medium Blue
⊿	827	Very Light Blue
☐		White

For baby's eyes, work French knots with 801 Dark Coffee Brown.

GASPAR ►

DMC #

☒	310	Black
�	322	Light Marine Blue
⊿	666	Bright Christmas Red
⊡	738	Very Light Tan
⊟	740	Tangerine
⊙	743	Dark Yellow

Outline robe and sleeves with 666 Bright Christmas Red, treasure box with 740 Tangerine.

JOSEPH ►

DMC #

◉	347	Dark Salmon
☐	{ 420	Dark Hazelnut Brown
	or	
	White	
⊡	754	Light Peach
☒	801	Dark Coffee Brown

Outline robe and sleeves with 347 Dark Salmon.

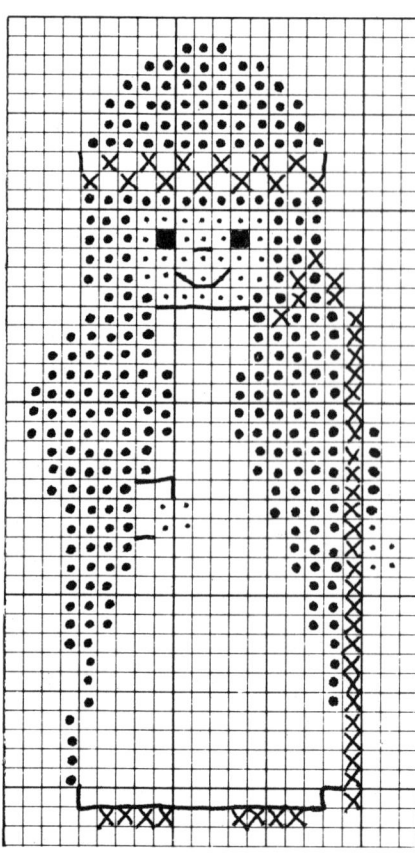

THE THREE KINGS

MELCHIOR ▶

DMC #

☒	310	Black
⊤	311	Medium Navy Blue
◉	702	Kelly Green
⊡	754	Light Peach
☐		White

Outline edges of White trim with 702 Kelly Green; outline sleeves with 310 Black.

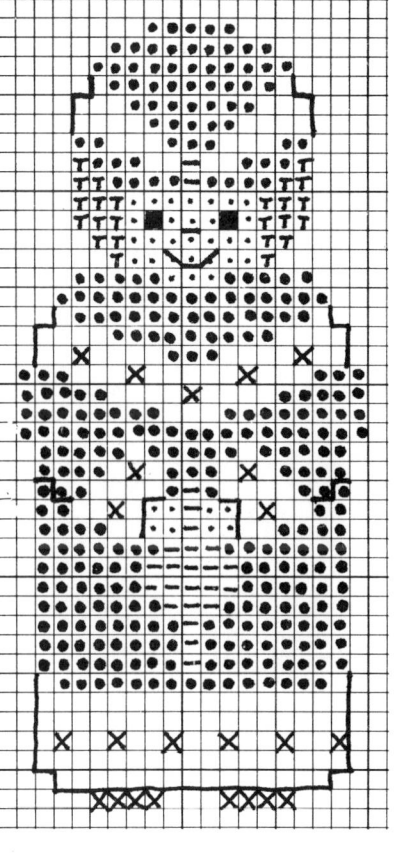

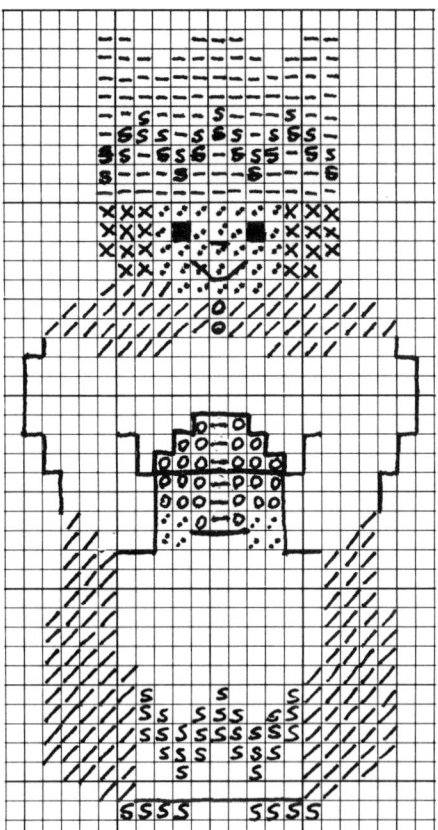

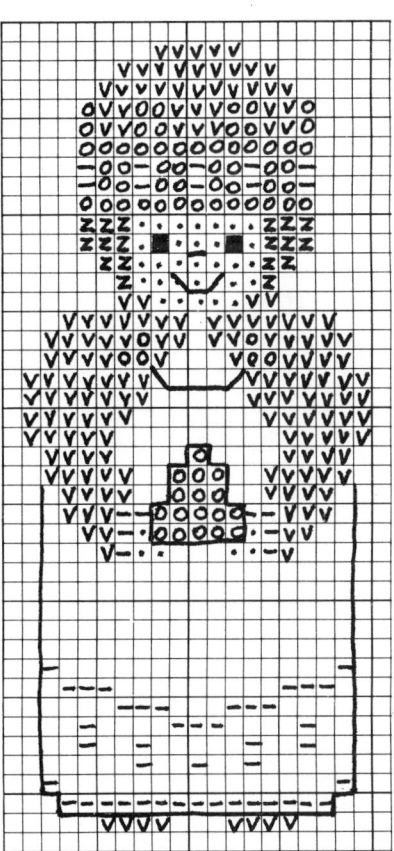

BALTHASAR ▶

DMC #

☑	553	Medium Violet
☒	647	Medium Beaver Gray
⊟	740	Tangerine
◎	743	Dark Yellow
⊡	754	Light Peach
☐		White

Outline robe and gift with 553 Medium Violet.

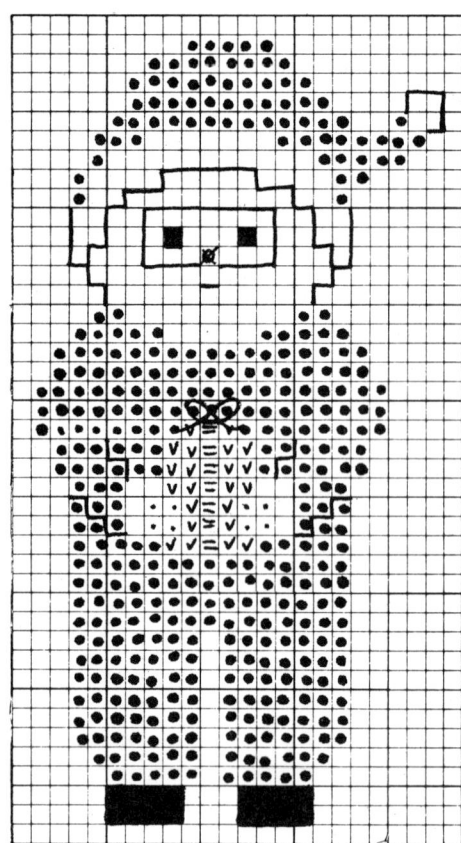

◄ SANTA CLAUS

DMC #

■	310	Black
◉	321	Christmas Red
⊠	321	Christmas Red French knot
▽	700	Bright Christmas Green
·	754	Light Peach
☐		White
⊟		Metallic Gold

Outline sleeves with White, cap and beard with 321 Christmas Red. For bow on package, thread needle with Metallic Gold. Leaving long ends of thread on front of work, insert needle into fabric on one side of a stitch at top of package and back out on other side of stitch; tie ends of thread in a bow.

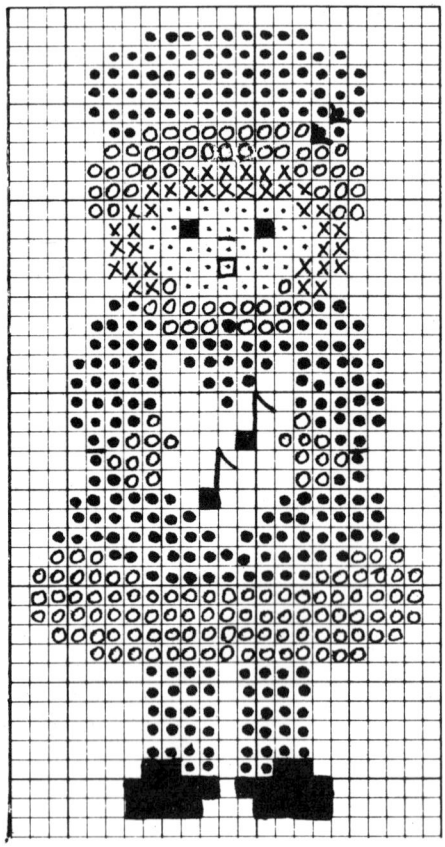

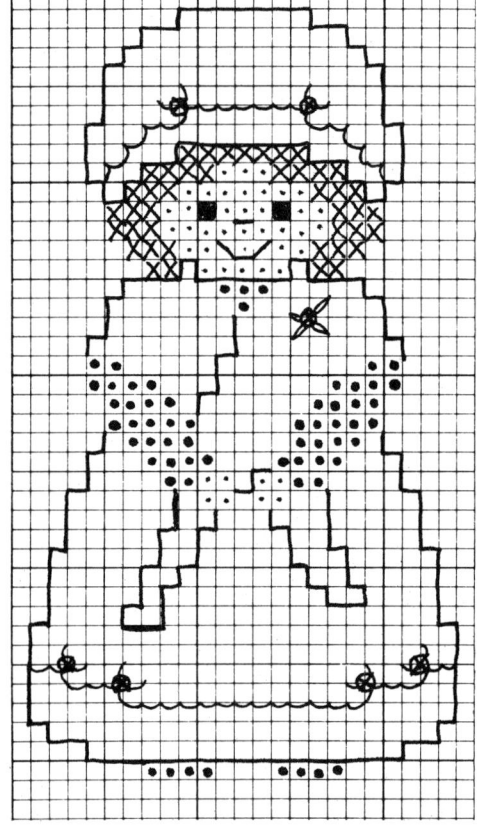

◄ MRS. SANTA

DMC #

⊠	318	Light Steel Gray
◉	321	Christmas Red
⊠	321	Christmas Red French knot
∼∼∼	700	Bright Christmas Green backstitch
·	754	Light Peach
☐		White

Outline dress, cap and shawl with 321 Christmas Red. With 700 Bright Christmas Green, work straight stitch leaves around each French knot.

GIRL ANGEL ▶

DMC #

■ 601 Dark Cranberry
□ ⎰ 962 Medium Dusty Rose
and ⎱   or
⊟ ⎱ 754 White
⊡ 840 Light Peach
☒   Medium Beige Brown
◎   Metallic Gold

Work robe in 962 Medium Dusty Rose or White; outline robe and work candle in the other color. Work trim on wings and robe in backstitch with 601 Dark Cranberry. For needlepoint, fill in space between halo and hair with White.

◀ CAROLER

DMC #

■ 310 Black
◉ 321 Christmas Red
☒ 433 Medium Brown
L 702 Kelly Green backstitch
⊡ 754 Light Peach
◎ 841 Light Beige Brown
□   White

Work stem and tail of each musical note in straight stitch with 310 Black.

DRUMMER BOY ▶

DMC #

■ 310 Black
◉ 321 Christmas Red
☑ 702 Kelly Green
⊡ 754 Light Peach
◪ 783 Christmas Gold
⊟ 824 Very Dark Blue
☒ 841 Light Beige Brown
□   White

Outline sleeves and jacket front with 824 Very Dark Blue. Work drum detail and drumsticks in straight stitch with 783 Christmas Gold.

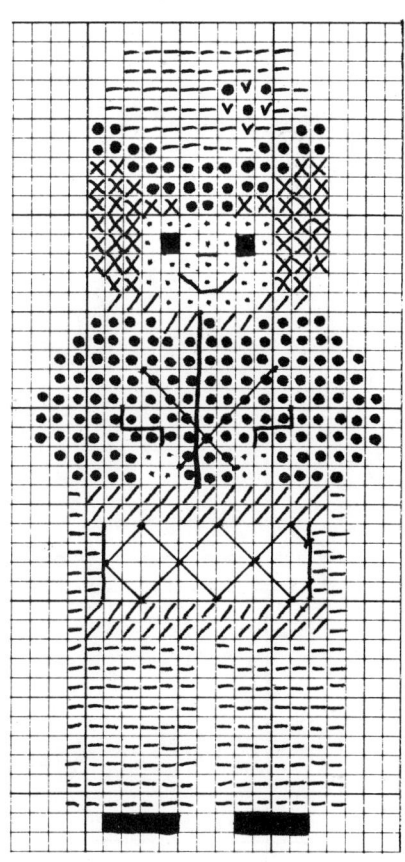

SIX STRAND EMBROIDERY COTTON (FLOSS) CONVERSION CHART

KEY: T = Possible Substitute   * = Close Match   — = No Match

DMC NO.	ROYAL MOULINÉ NO.	BATES/ANCHOR NO.
White	1001	2
Ecru	8600	926
208	3335*	110*
209	3415*	105
210	3320*	104
211	3410	108*
221	2570	897*
223	2555	894
224	2545	893
225	2540	892
300	8330	352*
301	8315*	349*
304	2415*	47*
307	6005*	289*
309	2525*	42*
310	1002	403
311	4275T	149*
312	—	147*
315	3130	896*
316	3120	895*
317	1030*	400*
318	1020*	399*
319	5025	246*
320	5015	216*
321	2415	47
322	—	978*
326	2530*	59*
327	3365*	101*
333	—	119
334	4250T	145
335	2525T	42*
336	4270*	149*
340	—	118
341	—	117
347	2425*	13*
349	2400	13
350	2045T	11
351	2015T	11*
352	2015	10*
353	2010*	8*
355	8095	5968
356	8090	5975*
367	5020	216*
368	5005*	240*
369	5005	213*
370	—	889*
371	—	888*
372	—	887*
400	8325*	351
402	8305*	347*
407	8005	882*
413	1025*	401
414	1020*	400*
415	1015	398
420	8720*	375*
422	8710*	373*
433	8265	371*
434	8215	309
435	8210*	369*
436	8205	363*

DMC NO.	ROYAL MOULINÉ NO.	BATES/ANCHOR NO.
437	8200*	362
444	6155*	291
445	6000	288
451	3415*	399*
452	—	399*
453	1015T	397*
469	5255	267*
470	5255*	267
471	5245	266*
472	5240	264*
498	2425T	20*
500	5125	879*
501	5120*	878
502	5110	876
503	5105	875
504	5100	213*
517	—	169*
518	4860*	168*
519	4855T	167*
520	—	862*
522	—	859*
523	—	859*
524	—	858*
535	1115T	401*
543	8500	933*
550	3380*	102*
552	3370*	101
553	3360	98
554	3355*	96*
561	—	212*
562	—	210*
563	—	208*
564	—	203*
580	5935	267*
581	5925	266*
597	4860*	168*
598	4855*	167*
600	2225*	59*
601	2225*	78*
602	2640*	77*
603	2720*	76*
604	2710	75*
605	2155	50*
606	7260	335
608	7255	333*
610	5825T	889*
611	5735T	898
612	8815*	832
613	5605*	956*
632	8530	936*
640	8625	903
642	8620*	392
644	8800	830
645	1115	905*
646	1115*	8581
647	1110	8581*
648	1100*	900
666	2405	46
676	6250	891
677	—	886*

DMC NO.	ROYAL MOULINÉ NO.	BATES/ANCHOR NO.
680	6260*	901
699	5375	923*
700	5365*	229
701	5365*	227
702	5330	239
703	5320	238
704	5310*	256*
712	8600*	387*
718	3015*	88
720	—	326
721	—	324*
722	—	323*
725	6215	306*
726	6150*	295
727	6135	293
729	6255	890
730	—	924*
731	—	281*
732	5925T	281*
733	—	280*
734	—	279*
738	8245*	942
739	8240*	885*
740	7045	316
741	6125	304
742	6120	303
743	6210	297
744	6110*	301*
745	6105	300*
746	6100	386*
747	4850	158*
754	8075	778*
758	8080	868
760	2035	9*
761	2030	8*
762	1010*	397
772	—	264*
775	4600*	128*
776	2110*	24*
778	3110	968*
780	8215*	310*
781	8215	309
782	6230	308
783	6220*	307
791	4165*	941*
792	4155T	940
793	4155	121
794	4145	120*
796	4340	133*
797	4265*	132*
798	4325	131*
799	4250*	130*
800	4310	128
801	8405	357*
806	4870T	169*
807	4860*	168*
809	4145*	130*
813	4610*	160*
814	2340T	44*
815	2530*	43

DMC NO.	ROYAL MOULINÉ NO.	BATES/ANCHOR NO.
816	2530	44*
817	2415T	19
818	2505*	48
819	2000	892*
820	4345	134
822	8605*	387*
823	4400*	150
824	4225	164*
825	4215	162*
826	4210	161*
827	4605	159*
828	4850	158*
829	5825	906
830	5825*	889*
831	5825T	889*
832	5815	907
833	5815*	874*
834	5810*	874
838	8425*	380
839	8560	380*
840	8555	379*
841	8550	378*
842	8505	376*
844	1115T	401*
869	8720*	944*
890	5025*	879*
891	2135	35*
892	2130	28
893	2125*	27
894	2115T	26
895	5430*	246*
898	8425*	360
899	2515	27*
900	7230*	333
902	—	72*
904	5295*	258*
905	5295	258*
906	5285*	256*
907	5280*	255*
909	5370	229*
910	5370*	228*
911	5465*	205*
912	5465	205
913	5460*	209
915	3030	89*
917	3020*	89*
918	8330*	341*
919	8095*	341*
920	8060*	339*
921	8060T	349*
922	8315T	324*
924	4830T	851*
926	4820*	779*
927	4810T	849*
928	1010T	900*
930	4510	922*
931	4505	921*
932	4500	920*
934	5070T	862*
935	5225T	862*

DMC NO.	ROYAL MOULINÉ NO.	BATES/ANCHOR NO.
936	5260T	269
937	5260	268
938	8430	381
939	4405	127
943	4935*	188*
945	8020*	347*
946	7230*	332*
947	7255*	330*
948	8070	778*
950	8020T	4146
951	8020T	366*
954	5455*	203*
955	5450	206*
956	2170*	40*
957	2160T	40*
958	—	187
959	—	186
961	2515*	76*
962	2515	76*
963	2505	49*
964	—	185
966	5150*	214*
970	7040	316*
971	7045	316
972	6120*	298
973	6015	290
975	8365	355*
976	8355	308*
977	8350	307*
986	5430	246*
987	5020*	244*
988	5295T	243*
989	5405T	242*
991	5165T	189*
992	4925*	187*
993	4915*	186*
995	4710	410
996	4700	433
3011	5525T	845*
3012	5525*	844*
3013	5515	842*
3021	5430	382*
3022	—	8581*
3023	—	8581*
3024	1100	900*
3031	—	905*
3032	8620T	903*
3033	8610*	388*
3041	3215*	871
3042	3205*	869
3045	6260T	373*
3046	5810	887*
3047	5805	886*
3051	5530T	846*
3052	5060T	859*
3053	5055*	859*
3064	8005*	914*
3072	4805*	397*
3078	6130	292*
3325	4200	159*

DMC NO.	ROYAL MOULINÉ NO.	BATES/ANCHOR NO.
3326	2115*	25*
3328	2045	11*
3340	—	329
3341	—	328
3345	5025T	268*
3346	5220T	257*
3347	5210*	266*
3348	5270*	265
3350	2220	42*
3354	2210	74*
3362	—	862*
3363	—	861*
3364	—	843*
3371	8435	382
3607	—	87*
3608	—	86
3609	—	85
3685	2335	70*
3687	2325	69*
3688	2320	66*
3689	2310	49
3705	—	35*
3706	—	28*
3708	—	26*
48	9000*	1201*
51	9014	1220
52	9006	1208
53	—	—
57	9002	1203
61	9013T	1218*
62	9000T	1201*
67	—	1211*
69	—	1218*
75	9002	1206*
90	9012T	1217*
91	9008*	1211
92	9011T	1216*
93	9007*	1210*
94	9011*	1216
95	9006T	1208*
99	9005*	1207*
101	9009*	1213*
102	—	1208*
103	—	1210*
104	9012	1217
105	9013*	1218*
106	9002T	1203*
107	9003	1204
108	9014*	1220*
111	9007*	1218*
112	9003T	1204*
113	9007*	1210*
114	9010	1215
115	9004	1206
121	9007	1210
122	9010T	1215*
123	—	1213*
124	9007T	1210*
125	9009	1213
126	9006*	1208*